T. W. (Theophilus Wilson) Moore

Treatise and Hand-book of orange Culture

In Florida, Louisiana and California

T. W. (Theophilus Wilson) Moore

Treatise and Hand-book of orange Culture
In Florida, Louisiana and California

ISBN/EAN: 9783337107000

Printed in Europe, USA, Canada, Australia, Japan

Cover: Foto ©ninafisch / pixelio.de

More available books at **www.hansebooks.com**

TREATISE AND HAND-BOOK

OF

ORANGE CULTURE

IN

FLORIDA, LOUISIANA AND CALIFORNIA.

BY

REV. T. W. MOORE, D.D.

FOURTH EDITION, REVISED AND ENLARGED

NEW YORK:
E. R. PELTON & CO.
1892.

CONTENTS.

	PAGE
Preface..	v
Chapter I.—The Profit of Orange Growing.................	11
Chapter II.—Of the Several Methods of Planting Orange Groves...	20
Chapter III.—The Wild Orange Grove Budded............	22
Chapter IV.—Groves from Transplanted Sour Stumps......	30
Chapter V.—Planting the Orange Seed.....................	36
Chapter VI.—Budding.......................................	41
Chapter VII.—On Selecting a Location for an Orange Grove..	47
Chapter VIII.—The Advantages of Partial Forest Shelter	54
Chapter IX.—"The Frost Line" and "The Orange Belt"	60
Chapter X.—The Effect of Frost on Plants.................	63
Chapter XI.—Transplanting.................................	68
Chapter XII.—The Distance Apart.........................	72
Chapter XIII.—Cultivation..................................	74
Chapter XIV.—Thorough Cultivation......................	79
Chapter XV.—Pruning......................................	85
Chapter XVI.—Fertilizing...................................	90
Chapter XVII.—Species, Varieties, etc......................	99
Chapter XVIII.—The Lemon and Lime.....................	116
Chapter XIX.—The Insects Damaging to the Orange Tree—The Natural Enemies of such Insects, and the Remedies to be Applied....................................	120

	PAGE
Chapter XX.—Diseases to which the Orange Tree and Fruit are Liable, and their Remedies	128
Chapter XXI.—Rust on the Orange	133
Chapter XXII.—Gathering, Packing, and Shipping the Orange	138
Chapter XXIII.—Crops that may be Grown Among the Orange Trees	144
Chapter XXIV.—Oils, Perfumes, Extracts, etc., from the Citrus	147
Chapter XXV.—Diseases of the Orange in Florida	149
Chapter XXVI.—Conclusion	157
Appendix	166

PREFACE.

SOME time before the discovery of America the sour orange—the brigerade—was introduced into Italy, and a short time thereafter it was carried to Spain. The Spaniards brought this variety to Florida. The sweet orange was then unknown in Europe. Doubtless the Spanish Catholic missionaries first distributed the seed of the brigerade—frequently called the Seville orange—in the vicinities of the Spanish forts and missions. As the fruit multiplied the seeds were scattered by the Indians along the banks of the rivers near their camping grounds, usually points projecting into the rivers. Thence they were scattered throughout the State of Florida.

The largest of these wild orange groves, twenty and fifty years ago, were found along the eastern and southern shores of rivers and lakes, and in the hammock and swamp lands of Florida. In addition to the protection from damage by the frost to the young plants, afforded by the water, the hammock and swamp lands gave protection against fires, which annually swept over the pine-woods, destroying the slow-growing trees. Some of these wild groves were, fifty years ago, cut down and the land cleared for planting corn, cotton, and cane. This was repeated as late as twenty-five years ago, before the monetary value of the orange was appreciated in this country.

One hundred years after America was discovered, the sweet orange was introduced into Europe. Later it was brought to Florida, and a few trees were planted in St. Augustine, and afterward in the settlements along the St. John's and Indian rivers. The pollen of the sweet orange fertilizing the flowers of the sour produced the hybrid " bittersweet." At the close of the Civil War, small plantations of sweet oranges were found throughout the State, consisting usually of a few trees growing around dwellings. There were a few groves of larger size, ranging from four hundred trees to nine hundred, in the vicinity of St. Augustine and along the St. John's River. The largest in the State were planted by Dr. Speer at Fort Reed, near Mellonville, and the Dummitt Grove on Indian River.

At the close of the war many of the old trees, both sweet and wild, were bearing liberal crops of such fruit as travellers from all parts of the world had never before eaten. The fruit sold at good prices. Some of those who had lately come into the State thought there was a living in an orange-grove. Land was bought, and planted in wild sour stumps. Seed-beds were planted for nursery stock, and acres were set with young plants. We were told that by the time our trees were ready to bear we would be in another country where there would be no need of planting. We answered then we would plant for our children. We were told that by the time the trees were in full bearing, oranges would not be worth picking in Florida. The evil prophecy failed. Other persons caught the orange fever, until finally the old prophets were converted, and are to-day our most enthusiastic orange-growers. To-day, hundreds of thousands of trees are growing, and tens of thousands more of plants are ready to be set in groves.

WILL THE BUSINESS BE OVERDONE?

The question now comes up, Will not the business be overdone? We answer, No. With the small area within the United States capable of producing oranges, this will be impossible. Canada and the United States are rapidly increasing in population, and these alone could consume the entire product from the orange-growing sections of the United States. But the Florida orange is the finest grown, and will ultimately command the market of Europe as well as America.

Occasionally already a glut in the market has occurred, but this has been in each instance the result of (mainly) a double fault on the part of the producers. They have attempted to narrow the marketing season to three or four months, when it should be extended over from eight to twelve months. Oranges will remain on the trees in good condition six months after they have turned yellow. Properly handled and cured, they will keep several months after they have been clipped. The Florida season for marketing, like the European, should embrace the entire year. The second mistake, to which allusion is made, was the result of the destructive hurry peculiar to Americans. The fruit was gathered green, carelessly handled, packed without being properly cured, much of it infested with fungi, and then gathered, packed, and shipped through all sorts of weather. Such fruit rapidly spoiled. Careless handling of transportation companies added to the disaster, and hence the merchants had to sell what sound fruit might reach them at low prices or throw it away.

Orange culture will pay beyond any other agricultural pursuit, even should the price fall to seventy-five cents per box. When reduced to that price fifty million boxes would not over-supply the present population of the United States and Canada. There are thirty States producing apples and peaches, and yet both these crops, which have to be marketed within a few weeks or months, are grown with profit. With such facts before us we have no fear as to the over-production of the orange.

A FASCINATING VOCATION.

To those engaged in the business, orange-growing is truly fascinating. The beauty of the tree, the beauty and fragrance of the flower, challenge all rivalry among ornamental trees and beautiful flowers. The æsthetic cultivator becomes a true lover of his sweet and beautiful pet, which he looks upon as a relic and reminder of Paradise. But when this beauty is accompanied with useful, golden, and gold-bearing fruit, affording a living, and promising all other material luxuries, then the lover appreciates his orange grove only less than he does his wife, who has brought to him not only the accomplishments of a sweet and cultivated woman, but with herself an ample fortune. And though he may have waited as long as Jacob did for his Rachel, he does not regret the toil and waiting, since the reward is ample. I do not know but that the toil and waiting demanded by the orange does not increase the ardor of the planter, and increase his pleasure when once the tree has been brought to full beauty and bearing, for we love best those that need to be courted earnestly in order to be won. When thus won we feel that the bride is the more fully our own.

HOW TO GROW THE ORANGE.

Does the reader wish to know how to win this fair bride clad in nature's richest green, adorned with golden globes, crowned with fragrant orange-blossoms—her own fair crown, so often plucked for other bridal wreaths?

The object of this book is to answer that inquiry. Growing oranges in Florida for profit is no longer a matter of experiment, as it was thought to be when the first edition of this treatise was published some years ago. The one million boxes shipped last season demonstrates the practicability of successfully growing oranges in Florida. The now known superiority of the Florida fruit is fast driving the foreign fruit out of the market, whenever and wherever the Florida orange is in the market. The successful shipping of oranges to Europe from Florida shows the practicability of enlarging the market indefinitely whenever the supply exceeds home consumption. The increased varieties, ripening early and late, a knowledge of the fact that the orange will continue to hang on the tree in good condition for months after it is ripe, that even after it has lost much of its juice in spring if allowed to remain on the tree it will again become as heavy and good as ever, the further knowledge that the fruit can be successfully kept for months by cold storage and other methods, show that the time of marketing can be lengthened several months, and probably throughout the year. The now known value and excellency of the Florida-grown lemon has doubled the possible capacity and value of the Florida-grown citrons.

Time and experience have further demonstrated to thousands who have been guided by the advice given in this little volume, that it is a safe guide for those who wish to engage in orange-growing. Scarcely a week passes without some expression of gratitude coming to the author from some one who has made a success in orange-growing by following the advice given in this book. To continue the publication is a necessity arising from the continued demand for the book.

With a hope that it may be of still further benefit to growers, this fourth edition is committed to an appreciating public by

THE AUTHOR.

FRUIT COVE, FLA.. August 30, 1885.

ORANGE CULTURE.

CHAPTER I.

THE PROFIT OF ORANGE-GROWING.

WHEN compared to the profit from other kinds of business, that derived from orange-growing is so large that a statement of facts is often withheld because the truth seems fabulous to those who have only had experience with other kinds of fruits. Those engaged in the business consider each tree, so soon as it is in healthy and vigorous bearing, worth one hundred dollars. Indeed the annual yield of such a tree will pay a large interest on the one hundred dollars—from ten to a hundred, and in some instances one hundred and fifty per cent per annum. Now if we take into consideration that from forty to one hundred trees are grown on an acre, the yield is immense. In the quiet country, breathing its pure atmosphere, with fresh fruits and vegetables from January to January, with milk, butter, honey, and poultry, the product of his farm and accessories to his grove, the man who has once brought his trees into successful bearing can enjoy all these and much more besides, having at his command an income quite equal to that commanded by owners of blocks of well-improved real estate in our towns and cities, with not one tenth part of the original cost of city investments. Or, if the owner chooses, he is at liberty to go abroad without fear of the incendiary's torch or the failure of commercial firms. And even if a frost should come severe enough to cut down full grown trees—and but one such frost has come in the history of Florida—the owner of such a grove has but to wait quietly for three years, and out of the ruin will come a second fortune as large as the first, and without the cost of brick, mortar, and workmen.

The age to which the orange tree lives, from three hundred to four hundred years, is so great that Americans do not know how to consider it in the light of a *permanent* investment. The fear has sometimes been expressed that the business will be overdone, that the supply will after a while exceed the demand, and the price of the fruit so decline that the orange will be unprofitable to the grower. But those who entertain this fear have certainly not considered the facts. The area of the States with climate suitable for growing the orange is comparatively small. The southern portion of California, a very small part of Louisiana, and the whole of Florida, if devoted to orange culture, is but a trifle compared to the vast sections of the United States which will be well filled with inhabitants long before the orange-growing sections can be brought into bearing. The present yield of fruit grown in the United States furnishes hardly one orange a year to each inhabitant. Our population will likely double, judging the future by the past, in the next thirty or forty years. To furnish such a population with one orange or lemon a day will require no less than thirty thousand millions of oranges or lemons per annum. The skill in gathering, curing, and packing the late and early varieties now appearing will enable the grower to furnish for the market at all seasons of the year either oranges or lemons. The wholesomeness of the fruit, together with its medicinal qualities, will increase its popularity as an article of food, until it will be universally used. At present the production of Florida oranges is so small that it is not known in the markets of many of our largest cities. The foreign varieties offered in those markets, even when fully ripe and eaten fresh in their own countries, will not compare with the Florida orange. But in order to reach this country in sound condition they have to be gathered when green, and hence are not only unpalatable but unwholesome. When the Florida orange becomes generally known, and the supply is adequate, it will exclude foreign fruit, and, because of its excellence, become universally used. Such will be the demand. Already successful shipments have been made to

Europe, which at no distant day is to get its best oranges in large quantities from Florida.

Now note the possibility of supply. Only a small proportion of those sections with climate sufficiently mild to grow the orange can ever be made available. A few of the more southern counties of California and that portion of Louisiana along the Gulf Coast can be made available for growing oranges profitably. In Florida the climatic conditions are more favorable, but the land and location suitable are not one hundredth part of the State. Another fact lessens the possibility of yield. Orange culture belongs to the class of *skilled* labor. Hundreds engaged in the business will fail, because success requires intelligence, application, patience, and skill. Hundreds have already failed, from one or all of these causes, and have left the State, never dreaming that they alone are to be blamed for their failure. Men in the very communities thus abandoned have succeeded because they were more prudent in the selection of soil and location, and used their intelligence and the intelligence of others, and persevered in the face of partial failure brought about by ignorance. But those men who failed took no advice except that of the landowner who offered to sell land cheaper than any one else. They read nothing that had been written by men who had succeeded. They took no warning of those who had failed. Stilted on their castle of self-conceit they stood, nor deigned to look down to the humble but *prudent* laborer for advice, till their castle fell, and they left the State imagining that the "sand of Florida" had proven an unstable foundation and overthrown them and their castle. Such instances will repeat themselves. Whoever may succeed, such men will fail. Whatever may be written, and wisely written on the subject, and however published, whether in book or journal, will not be read by them. But while the above facts will lessen the general yield of oranges, it will make the business vastly more profitable to the men who possess the virtues necessary to success. The orange will pay beyond any other fruit at half a cent an orange on the tree. In Europe, where lands are exceedingly high, a grove is considered a most profitable investment, even when the fruit sells at from two dollars to four dollars per thousand. Ten years ago the Florida orange was considered well sold when the grower could get one cent on the tree. Few now sell for less than one and a half cent, and some average at their groves as high as four cents per orange, and the price still advances.

In no business can a young man with pluck, intelligence, and application, so certainly lay the foundation for a competency and fortune as in orange-growing in Florida. With the exercise of these he may in ten years be what the country would call a rich man.

A young man from Middle Florida borrowed

money enough from his father to buy a piece of land. After paying for his land, located a few miles above Palatka, he landed in Palatka with three dollars in his pocket. These he paid for provisions, and went to work growing vegetables on about an acre and a half of cleared land. Six years afterward he sold his place for twelve thousand dollars cash, without owing a cent for anything. Many instances could be given of young men, as well as old men, who have done as well, and of some who have done still better. Young men have frequently written to the author to aid in securing for them a clerkship. His advice has been invariably given, " Go to work raising fruit in Florida, and be *independent* and *have a home.*"

ORANGE CULTURE IN CALIFORNIA.

We clip the following statistics of making an orange grove in California from the address of Mr. L. M. Holt, Secretary of the Southern California Horticultural Society. It will be observed that the rates are far above those charged in Florida in some of the items, land for one :

" An orange orchard in full bearing will yield 100,000 oranges to the acre. Five dollars per thousand will pay all the expenses of taking care of the orchard and picking and marketing the crop in San Francisco, or to any other market to which the freights are no greater. If the price should come down from the present figure to ten dollars per 1000—jobbing rates—there will still be left five dollars per 1000, or five hundred dollars per acre for the producer, which on a ten-acre tract will satisfy the cupidity of the most avaricious. There is scarcely a possibility that the price of good clean oranges will reach so low a figure as ten dollars per thousand yet, for years to come.

WHAT WILL IT COST TO GET SUCH AN ORCHARD?

"As a guide to those who may desire to figure on the probable expense of starting an orange orchard. I give below some figures which are applicable to Riverside ; they must be changed somewhat for other localities. Land in Riverside settlement is comparatively high. One year ago good wild land could be obtained for seventy-five dollars per acre, and even at sixty dollars per acre under the canals. To-day there is none for sale at a less figure than one hundred and fifty dollars per acre, and choice land in good locations is held at two hundred dollars per acre firm. Lower priced lands can be had in other localities, and in no place in Southern California does it command as high a figure as here in Riverside. In applying these figures to other localities the price of land can be figured all the way from twenty-five to one hundred dollars per acre. Following are the figures for a ten-acre tract :

COST.

Ten acres of land in Riverside	$1500
One thousand trees, budded or seedling	750
Planting and caring for same first season, at twenty-five dollars per acre	250
Caring for orchard second year, at fifteen dollars per acre	150

Third year, fifteen dollars per year.............	150
Fourth year, twenty dollars per acre............	200
Fifth year, twenty-five dollars per acre..........	250
Other expenses incidental to work..............	550
Total for five years........................	$3800
Interest on investment.....................	1200
Total	$5000

"This is the expense account. There will be some receipts. If good budded trees are planted, the third year will give a little fruit, the fourth year still more, and at the end of the fifth year there will be quite a fine crop. In order to be safe in these calculations we will place the yield and prices at the lowest possible estimate:

Third year crop, scattering oranges—a few hundred or thousand—not counted.	
Fourth year, an average of fifty oranges to the tree—50,000 oranges at twenty dollars per thousand...................................	$1000
Fifth year, 200 to the tree—200,000 oranges at twenty dollars per thousand............	4000

"If these prices are maintained the owner has his investment all back again at the end of five years, and is ready to ship oranges in large quantities every year thereafter.

"All persons planting orange orchards do not do as well as this, and some do better. Those figures represent what can be done with good judgment and thorough work. If a man thinks to save by getting cheap and incompetent work, he may succeed in reducing the cost a few dollars, and the receipts a few hundred dollars, or even a few thousand dollars. If he buys a poor tree he can get it for twenty cents, instead of paying the market price for a good thrifty tree, he will make another saving in cost of orchard, and in cost of boxes in which to ship the fruit."

CHAPTER II.

OF THE SEVERAL METHODS OF PLANTING ORANGE GROVES.

THE question is frequently asked, "Which is the best?" The several methods are—1st, the budding of the wild sour trees without moving them; 2d, budding them first and planting afterward in some suitable location; 3d, planting the sour stumps and budding afterward; 4th, growing the trees from sweet seed without budding; 5th, planting the sweet seedling and budding either before or after removal from nursery; 6th, budding on sour seedlings either before or after removal from nursery; and 7th, a grove of sweet seedlings.

Each of these plans has some advantage over the others. They all have advocates, but which of all has the greatest number of advantages is questionable. I have tried them all; but, after stating the advantages of each, must leave to the grower to select for himself as circumstances and inclination may control.

If one is impatient for returns, let him choose the sour grove, if he can find it, and bud the trees where they stand. With proper management he may begin to gather in two years. If he is still impatient but cannot find a sour grove, let him buy the sour stumps, plant them in some suitable location, and he may begin to gather fruit in three years from planting. But if he can wait a while longer for fruit, with the hope of getting a longer-lived tree and more abundant yield, let him plant *younger* trees, either seedlings or budded stock. If he wishes an early bearer and comparatively smaller tree, he can select the *sour* seedling budded. If a larger but later bearer, he can select the *sweet* seedling budded. If he wishes an abundant yield and the largest trees, and can wait a longer time, the sweet seedling unbudded will suit. With good treatment such trees will begin to yield in eight years, and after a longer time, in ninety-nine cases out of a hundred, give him a fair quality of fruit; but perhaps he will have as many varieties or sub-varieties as trees in his grove. The sour stock for a few years grows more rapidly, but will finally make a smaller tree than the sweet. The best quality of fruit can be insured only by budding from the best varieties.

As to the relative advantages of seedling and budded trees, each year's experience and observation increase my appreciation of budded trees. Were I to plant again, I think I would plant no other.

CHAPTER III.

THE WILD ORANGE GROVE BUDDED.

THIS grove yields so readily under so simple treatment that we shall consider it at once. Of course nature has already determined the location, and in many instances the location has been wisely chosen, not only with reference to best protection from frost, but also in many instances with reference to cheap and easy transportation, on the banks of navigable rivers and creeks. Wherever a wild grove can be found so located, the purchaser can afford to pay a liberal price if he has to buy, or the owner can afford to improve by the most approved methods.

Many, however, have been the blunders made in attempts to improve such valuable property. I know of many groves greatly damaged, and some completely sacrificed, by bad management. The two mistakes most frequently made in the treatment of such groves are, first, the reckless destruction of the forest trees furnished by nature for the protection of the orange, and, second, the continued pulling off of the young shoots from the stumps cut off for the purpose of budding. The first and second buds having failed, the cultivator continues to reduce the vitality of the tree by pulling off the young shoots, until at last the sap, for want of elaboration through the leaf, becomes diseased, and the tree, tenacious of life as it is, dies of the double cause of exhaustion and disease. It may be well to caution the orange-grower at once against the commission or repetition of this frequent blunder. Few of our forest trees will survive being cut down to a stump; still fewer will survive if the young shoots are kept down for a few months. Every time the young shoots are pulled off, the young rootlets, corresponding to and starting at the same instant with the shoots, die, and the effort of nature to restore vitality is checked and weakened until the hardiest tree is soon killed. In budding *old* stumps I have found it of great advantage to allow a few shoots to grow along the trunk, *below* the bud, pinching back these shoots, allowing a few leaves on each shoot to grow to full size, and so furnishing the tree with healthy sap, encouraging the development and maturity of new wood and new roots, and keeping up an active circulation. Continue this until the sweet bud has so far advanced as to be able to furnish the tree with sufficient leaf to enable it to collect sufficient carbon from the atmosphere to insure the health of the tree. After this point has been reached you may then pluck off all the sour shoots and keep them off. In some instances where a sweet bud has made an early start, a more vigorous growth of the sweet bud may be obtained by plucking off all the sour shoots from the first, but this is at the risk of the health of both the stock and the bud. I will mention one other thing in this connection : do not allow the sweet bud to grow too long before pinching it back. If allowed to grow two or three feet, as it will from a very vigorous stump, it is liable to be broken off by the wind. But even if it should be securely tied so as to prevent such an accident, it should, nevertheless, be pinched back in order to hasten the maturity of its own wood and leaves. The *mature* leaves are necessary to the health of both stock and bud, and necessary to gain a controlling influence over the circulation, and to draw it as early as possible to the sweet bud. By this means also the mature wood of the sweet bud is better enabled to resist the blighting influence of both sun and frost. Still another advantage is gained. By pinching back the bud it is induced to branch near its junction with the stock and thus enlarge and strengthen its connection with the stock.

I again call the attention of the reader to the other mistake mentioned in the beginning of this chapter, and so frequently made by those who have undertaken to improve wild groves. Nature has not only planted these groves, found above the frost line on the south side of bodies of water, but has also taken the additional precaution to plant them under the protection of forest trees. Thus doubly guarded, these orange trees have grown, some of them probably for a century. As the cold winds from the north-west have swept down upon them, the frost has been tempered by passing over a body of water of higher temperature than the winds. The spreading branches of forest trees, hanging like canopies, have checked the radiation of heat passing from the surface of the earth, and inclosed the orange grove in a vapor bath. And even if the tempest has been too strong and cold, and swept away the warm air-blanket thrown by nature over the tender orange shoot, and the cold has frozen the sap until the tender woody tissues have been ruptured, still the forest trees have stood like foster-mothers to keep off the rays of the morning sun till these ruptured tissues and sap vessels could be healed by the efforts of nature. The mother who has suddenly plunged the body of her scalded child into a bath of flour or oil to save the child from suffering and death, has not shown a tenderer care than the forest trees have extended for scores of years over their charges. And yet the first thing done by many of us who wished to *improve* our wild groves was to cut down these natural protectors to a tree. The wonder is, not that so many of these wild groves have been destroyed, but that any have been saved after such abuse.

But we will not now discuss the advantages of partial forest protection. The subject is of too much importance to be dismissed in a single paragraph. We will consider this subject in a separate chapter further along. I have thus early noticed this subject lest the reader may do what I and hundreds of others have done—*destroy* these magnificent wild groves when attempting to improve them.

Before beginning to bud a wild orange grove, first cut down all the underbrush, and then the smaller forest trees. This rubbish can be removed or burned and the ashes used as fertilizer for the orange trees, spreading a liberal quantity around the trunks to keep off the " wood-lice"—white ants—which frequently attack trees where there is much rubbish left on the ground. Or, if lime can be had, sprinkle this around the trunks and let the rubbish rot on the ground. The decayed brush will add greatly to the fertility of the soil and will soon be out of the way. It would add greatly, however, to the ease with which you accomplish your subsequent work to take all this rubbish out of the way.

The ground cleared of underbrush and small trees, pass through and select at suitable intervals the forest trees you wish to remain. Select a plenty of these trees, and mark them so that they will not be cut down. If afterward they are found standing too thickly on the ground, some of them can be felled. If felled too hastily, fifty years cannot restore them. The number of these trees which are to remain is to be determined by circumstances. If the place is well protected by water, fewer trees will answer. But be certain to leave enough trees to keep off the morning sun after a frost, as it is the sudden thawing more than the freeze which kills the trees. Trees intended for shelter should be of habits the opposite of those of the orange. You wish the orange to have low-spreading branches. Select as their protectors trees so tall that their lower branches will not interfere with the foliage of the orange. The orange tree sends most of its roots near the surface of the ground. Select as their protectors trees that send their roots deep. I have noticed several varieties of live oak in the State. Only one of these is in the habit of sending its roots deep into the soil. Whenever I have found this variety growing I could plant the orange close to its trunk without damage to the orange. The persimmon has this habit of deep feeding, but unfortunately it drops its foliage in the winter. The pine has this habit only when grown in a well-drained soil. There are some individual trees whose habits are an exception to the general habits of the variety. These can soon be discovered by the use of the spade or hoe. But if trees without surface feeders cannot be found, then select trees with other desirable qualities and cut the surface roots by a trench ten or twelve inches deep a few feet from and around the base. After those trees have been selected and marked which you wish to remain, you can now cut next such trees as can be felled without damage to the standing orange trees. The work thus far should be done during the fall or winter, so as to be ready for the spring and summer work which is to follow.

In early spring, before the new growth of the orange has started, begin to saw off the limbs of the orange trees if they branch near the ground, taking off all the top. If the trunks are long, cut off the tree, leaving about two and a half feet of stump. Immediately afterward fell the balance of the forest trees that are to be cut.

So soon as the sap begins to flow freely, and the bark to break by the springing of new shoots, insert sweet "sprig" buds, ranging from the top to six inches below the top of the stump, inserting four or more buds to the tree. I have sometimes hastened the development of the bud by inserting the bud before cutting off the top, if the sap was flowing freely, and so soon as the bud was known to be living then cutting off the top. But this has been with trees standing apart from others. Where they stand thickly, as is generally the case in the wild grove, the felling of the tops usually knocks out or so disturbs the bud as to cause it to die.

As the young sour shoots start, rub off all above and in the immediate vicinity of the buds. Allow a few shoots to remain along the trunk, but pinch them back after growing a few inches. Be careful to allow none to reach higher than the bud, as the tendency of the sap is to flow in greatest abundance to the highest point. I have already mentioned some advantages to be derived from first allowing sour shoots to grow and then pinching them back. I mention one other advantage. This method soon furnishes new and mature wood on which to bud if the first buds fail.

After the sweet buds have grown ten or twelve inches, pinch back, simply taking out the terminal bud. So soon as the buds have started fairly a second growth, you may begin to lessen the quantity of the sour shoots below, until you can safely risk the tree's health with the foliage furnished by the sweet bud. You may have to occasionally pinch back the sweet bud. It is safest to hold it in such check as will hasten the *maturity* of wood, and *thickness* rather than length of branches.

In the after-cultivation of such groves, if the deposit of leaves is sufficient to keep down the grass, do not disturb the soil with plow or hoe for the first year or two. Pull up or cut down with a scythe any weeds that may spring up. I believe such groves can be most economically and successfully cultivated by keeping up nature's method. I have had several letters of inquiry as to the proper cultivation of such groves, correspondents dwelling upon the difficulties of plowing and hoeing while roots were so near the surface.

CHAPTER IV.

GROVES FROM TRANSPLANTED SOUR STUMPS.

THE next most expeditious way of getting a sweet grove is from transplanted stumps of sour trees. It is sometimes the case that persons improving wild groves, having budded all the trees and finding them too thickly set on the ground, will sell those budded stumps at a fair price. When this is the case a grove can be brought into bearing in a short time. I have frequently had such trees to fruit the same year of planting. But this has been the case only where they have been taken up with great care, with abundance of root, and removed but a short distance. But even where this early fruiting *can* be secured, the policy is doubtful. The tree should not be taxed with efforts to bear fruit so early after its removal and in its enfeebled condition. It requires much greater effort on the part of the tree to bear fruit than to produce new wood. One of these budded sour stumps of medium size, carefully taken up with good roots and carefully cultivated, will begin the second year to bear considerable fruit, if it has not been allowed to fruit the year of planting. The third year such a tree will begin to pay a good interest on the investment of purchase-money.

There are some objections to a grove of this kind. These trees from old stumps never grow to be so large as the unbudded seedlings, nor bear so abundantly. They are believed also to be much shorter lived. European writers tell us such is the case, but I do not believe that our experience in Florida has been of sufficient length to test the age to which one of these trees will live and bear fruit. Some of the oldest bearing trees in this State, of such origin, are still fine bearers and in vigorous health. One other objection I will mention. It is generally believed that it is hard to make the old stumps live. The sad experience of those of us who, a few years ago, bought such stumps by the hundred and had them die almost as fast as they were set, has made this kind of business very unpopular. But I am persuaded that most of this disaster can be attributed to ignorance and carelessness. I am satisfied now that if I had handled sweet seedlings as I and every one else then handled sour stumps, the sweet seedlings would have died almost as badly. There is no doubt that the younger the tree the less risk there is in removing it. But the early return to be gathered from these sour stumps, budded either before or after removal, will justify the risk in planting a few in every new grove, and if the stumps can be bought at a fair price and are near at hand, so as not to be damaged in transporting them, the grower would do well to plant them liberally. In transplanting sour stumps too much care cannot be exercised.

Many of the wild groves are found in low wet land. The tap-root is small, and the laterals near the surface, while reaching a considerable distance, have few or no fibrous roots near the base of the tree. They have also been accustomed to an abundance of shade and moisture. One must see at once that new and entirely different habits must be formed by such trees transplanted into a drier soil and with less shade and moisture. These new habits have to be formed at a time when the tree is least able to bear the change. It is better to select trees grown in a drier soil. I have, however, succeeded in transplanting trees from a swamp, at the time of taking them up flooded with water. Some such are now healthy and fine bearers.

In taking up large sour trees, have at hand a sharp axe, a sharp narrow-bladed saw, and two sharp spades prepared especially for such work. The spades should be made to order, narrower than usual, with handle and jaws sufficiently stout to be used in prying. With such tools the work will be greatly expedited and done much more satisfactorily. The time saved in one day's work with such tools will pay for their cost.

If ready to begin, saw off the top, leaving a stump five or six feet high to be used as a lever for bending the tree out of its bed. Now drive down the spade, cutting the roots in a circle two feet and a half from the base or trunk. Shake the tree to see if all the lateral roots have been cut. If not it will be necessary to cut a trench the width of the spade to enable you to cut deeper. In making the second cut incline the point of the spade toward the tap-root. Next cut the tap-root two feet and a half from the surface and lift the stump from its bed. Place the stumps at once in the shade and wrap them well with wet green moss. Protect as far as possible from the sun and drying winds. After taking a stump from the soil plant it in position as soon as possible. One great cause of failure has arisen from keeping them out of the ground too long, and allowing the roots to be exposed to wind and sun.

In setting, have the holes freshly dug. Do not allow the soil to dry before it is replaced around the roots. Dig the holes, for resetting, five feet wide and ten or twelve inches deep. If the holes are dug too deep it is almost impossible to keep the tree from sinking too deep in its position, as the fresh soil settles. In the centre of the hole dig a deeper hole the width of the spade for the tap-root. With a sharp knife, and where the roots are too large for the knife, with a sharp saw with fine teeth, cut away all fractures and bruises from the ends of roots. So set the tree that it will stand, after the soil has been settled by showers, a little higher than it stood in its original bed. It had better be higher by two inches than lower by one inch than it originally grew. You cannot be too cautious at this point. If the tree is set too deep, it may live, but it will not flourish for some time ; it may be not for years, but certainly not till it has sent out fresh surface roots to take the place of those which have been smothered by having been buried too deeply. The tree having been put in position, replace the soil, packing it first firmly around the tap-root. Now press down the ends of the laterals so that they will have a slight dip, and fill in with soil, treading it firmly upon the roots. Finally cover over with two inches of light soil and leave the ground level. When the ground is sufficiently wet it is not necessary to use water. But if the ground is dry, use enough water to settle the soil firmly around the roots, and especially around the tap-root, but do not wet the top layer of earth. •I prefer planting after showers to using water. If the planting is done in spring or summer, mulch at once with one or two inches of litter, and if the trees have been set in the open ground shelter them from the sun by setting a pine bough to the south of the tree. If the stumps have been taken from a dry soil the above is sufficient to insure their living, but if taken from a very wet soil, be careful to keep the ground moist till the new roots have well started and penetrated well into the soil. The stump should be cut off two and a half feet high. If the stumps have been budded, and the buds have grown to considerable length, cut them back, leaving here and there a few leaves to direct the current of the sap into the sweet wood. If the stumps have not been budded, so soon as the bark begins to break with new shoots and separate freely from the wood, insert three or four sprig buds near the top, and treat the tree as directed in budding the natural grove. Fertilizers should not be added till the trees are well established. When fertilizers are applied, do not place them near the trunk and above the roots, but a little beyond their extremity.

CHAPTER V.

PLANTING THE ORANGE SEED.

IN selecting seed for the nursery, if you intend budding the young trees, you need not be careful as to the quality of fruit from which the seed is taken. The plant from the sour seed, as already stated, will for a few years grow more rapidly, but make a smaller tree than the plant from the sweet fruit.

If you desire to grow your trees without budding, select only from the best fruit, and from trees not grown in the vicinity of any trees bearing sour or indifferent fruit. All the varieties and even species of the *citrus* family mix very readily, and if grown in close proximity, seeds from the same tree will give an endless variety of fruits, the tendency, however, being toward the kind produced by the tree from which the fruit is plucked, as the pistils are more apt to be fertilized by pollen from flowers near at hand.

If sour seed are to be planted, the fruit may be thrown into piles till rotted and the seed washed out from the pulp. But whatever kind is used, do not allow the seed to dry. Put them at once into moist sand, to be kept till ready for planting.

The seeds may be planted either in boxes, or in the open ground, or under glass, as quantity or other circumstances may suggest. If fruit is eaten in the early winter, the seed may at once be planted in boxes and the boxes set in some warm place indoors, and the plants be so far advanced as to be ready to set in the nursery early in the spring.

In preparing beds or boxes for seed, have the bottom soil covered two or three inches deep with fresh leaf mould from the hummock. Place the seeds about one inch apart and cover with half an inch of soil—leaf mould. Finish by a covering of one inch of mulching and a thorough watering. Keep the soil moist, but not wet. If the seed-bed is in the open ground it is well to hold the mulching in place by laying a few brush on the bed.

I have sometimes succeeded very well by allowing the seed to remain in a box of sand till they have started to sprout and then planting them directly in the nursery. In this case select a place partially sheltered by forest trees. Prepare the soil thoroughly for ten or twelve inches deep. Open the rows four feet apart and eight inches deep. Fill to within two inches of the top with well-rotted muck, drop the seed three inches apart, and cover with one and a half inch of soil.

In selecting a position for the nursery, if your place is well protected by water on the cold points you may risk your nursery in the open field. But if you are not satisfied about the protection, select a position sheltered from the morning sun, to prevent the too sudden thawing after a frost. I would prefer shade on the south as well, as the sun sometimes breaks out suddenly during a cold snap about noon. Under such circumstances I have known serious damage done to young plants. A still better plan is to clear away a half or a quarter of an acre of ground in the midst of a tall forest. Around this half acre or quarter acre sink a ditch two feet deep, in order to cut the surface roots of the forest trees. Plow or spade the land deep. Open the rows four feet apart and eight or ten inches deep, fill them with good muck or leaf mould clear of such litter as would attract wood-lice. Over this muck place an inch or two of soil to keep the muck moist. A dressing of ashes or slaked lime will be of advantage, especially if the muck has not been previously well rotted in heaps. Your land can now stand till the trees are ready to be taken from the seed-bed. Some prefer putting the muck, or whatever fertilizer is used, broadcast over the land. But my reason for advising the muck to be put in drills is that if well rotted it will not heat, but will serve to keep the roots of the young plant in a compact body. A great deal is saved by this means when you come to transplant to the grove; the roots having grown in a compact body, very little will be lost by root-pruning. And where the distance from the nursery to the grove is short, and the transplanting is done when the ground is wet, the entire ball of muck may be taken along with and adhering to the roots, and the tree hardly feel the shock of the removal. When the young plants in the seed-beds are a few inches high and have four or five leaves, they may be transplanted to the nursery. In taking them up, cut off the ends of the tap-roots so that they will not be apt to double up in setting them. The setting is better done in rainy weather. The ground should be thoroughly wet in order to insure a good result. The rows can now be opened four or five inches deep, and the young plants dropped at a distance of six inches apart. Let a hand follow, and before the roots have time to dry set them in an upright position, carefully spreading out the roots and packing the soil around them. Be careful not to set the plants deeper than they grew in the seed-beds. When a row or two have been set, level off the ground with a rake, leaving the sandy soil on the surface and not the muck, as the latter hardens under the influence of the sun. If a shower does not follow soon, it is well to water, in order to settle the earth well around the roots. If the sun is hot, a little shade for a few weeks would be beneficial. Pine boughs can be laid over the ground, or palmetto leaves stuck along the rows. The nursery should be thoroughly worked and kept clear of weeds and grass, and the soil frequently stirred to the depth of two inches.

Eight or ten months before removing the plants

from the nursery, root-prune the young plants. This can be done by pushing a sharp spade eight or ten inches deep on each side, and six inches from the rows. This can be done more expeditiously by placing a revolving cutter on a plow to be drawn by a horse. This method of root-pruning has all the advantage of replanting, with the additional advantage of great saving of labor and little check to the growing plants.

CHAPTER VI.

BUDDING.

WHERE it is the purpose of the orange-grower to bud his trees it is better that the budding should be done before the trees are taken from the nursery. The reasons are—1st, the sooner in the life of the tree the budding is done the earlier and more thorough the healing of the wounds; 2d, the budding is done with greater ease and rapidity in the nursery than in the grove; 3d, in transplanting trees of considerable size it is impossible to take up all the roots, and as it is necessary that the top should not exceed in proportion the roots in transplanting trees, it is beneficial to cut back the top considerably. If the budding has been done but a few months before transplanting, the wounds will have healed and the proportion between the roots and top will have become about right for transplanting without the necessity of inflicting new wounds upon the branches at a time when the tree is in its most tender condition.

A good time to begin to bud is when the trees in the nursery are one year old. By budding every alternate tree the budded trees can be set the following season, leaving greater space for larger growth of the trees left in the nursery. Those remaining can be budded when two years old and set the season following. Where trees are to be bought from the nurseryman it is preferable to plant trees older than one or two years, as older trees come into bearing sooner. But where persons are growing their own stock, the sooner they are set, after the first year, in position, the more rapidly they will grow, if the trees are properly cultivated.

In budding nursery stock, but one plan, that of inserting a single bud, is practised. The graft has not done well. Grafted trees will live, but they do not grow so thriftily as the budded tree. Grafting is sometimes resorted to when one wishes to preserve a new variety, and he has obtained a cutting of this new variety in winter when the sap is not in condition for budding. Sprig budding is not resorted to for nursery stock, as the stem is usually too small to admit the sprig. Do not attempt to bud except when the sap is flowing freely—so freely that the bud will readily lift the bark as you push it downward into its position. The stock to be budded should be trimmed so as to have as few as possible of branches or leaves in the way of the operator. The trimming should be done several days beforehand, so that the wounds may be in a healing condition and the flow of sap not checked by too much cutting at the time of budding. The budding-knife should be sharp, that it may *cut* through the hard wood of the bud without splitting the fibre of the wood or bark.

Select buds from healthy and vigorous trees of the variety to be propagated. They should not be too old or they will be slow in starting, nor too young lest they perish. The wood from which they are taken should be nearly mature, between the angular and the round. Select buds with well-developed eyes. It is sometimes the case that insects have eaten out the eyes. It is useless to put in such buds. In cutting the bud from the branch, do not hold the blade of the knife at right angles with the branch, as in such a position it is likely to slip in and out, following the grain of the wood, and so giving an uneven surface to the face of the bud. The face of the bud should be so level and straight that when it is pushed into its position the cut surface will at all points touch the wood of the stock and so exclude the air. To prevent this irregularity of surface, hold the blade of the knife firmly in the hand and almost parallel with the branch from which the bud is being cut. In cutting, draw the knife to you, as the cut will be smoother by this method than if the bud were severed from the branch by simply pressing the blade through the wood. The knife should be inserted half an inch above the bud and come out a half or three quarters of an inch below. It is better to insert the bud on the north side of the stock. The incision in the stock should be made with a downward cut and about three fourths of an inch long. At the top of this incision make a cross incision, each time only cutting through the bark. With the point of the knife, turning the back of the blade to the wood so as not to dull the blade, raise the bark at the top of and on either side of the first incision, so as to enable you to insert and push down the bud. If the sap is flowing freely the bud in its downward motion will easily lift the bark, and as it takes its position exclude the air from beneath it and the wood of the stock. After the bud has been pushed partly down with the fingers, place the blade of the knife one fourth of an inch above the eye of the bud and perpendicular to the line of the first incision, press the knife through the bark of the bud, and by a downward motion force the bud down till the knife comes directly over the second incision. Tie in the bud with strips of cloth a quarter or a half inch wide, or, what is better, with strings of woollen yarn, as its elasticity will not allow the strangling of the bud so soon. In tying do not bring the cloth or string in contact with the eye of the bud. So wrap as to hold the bud firmly in its place, and to exclude the rain if any should fall soon after budding. Revisit the buds eight or ten days after they have been inserted. If they are living, take the wrapping from that part of the bud below the eye. The wrapping above the eye may be loosened, but it should not be taken off so soon. Where the bud is living, cut off the stock three or four inches above. As the bud grows it should be tied to this upper section of the stock for support. After the bud has started on its second growth, if the stock is small it should then be cut off just above the bud ; if larger, a longer time should be allowed before cutting off the stock close to the bud.

Before leaving this subject, attention is called to the importance of having the top of the bud fit neatly against the bark above. The law governing the growth of trees is this : the sap passing upward through the pores of the sap-wood is elaborated through the leaf. It is only after the new sap has entered the leaf and absorbed carbon from the atmosphere that it is ready to make new wood. The sap having secured its carbon descends the tree mainly between the bark and the wood. As it descends evaporation is carried on through the pores of the bark, and the thickened sap makes a deposit along the line of its descent and around the trunk of the tree just under the bark. This thickened sap presently hardens into wood. It is this fact, that new wood is generally formed by this *downward* flow of sap, which makes it so important that the top of the bud should come in close contact with the *upper* bark. Placed thus it is put in contact with and in the way of the direct current of life. Placed otherwise, its chance of life is dependent upon lateral circulation or absorption.

If the buds are from the Mandarin or Tangerine varieties, insert them during spring or autumn, as they do not live readily when inserted during the heat of summer.

CHAPTER VII.

SELECTING A LOCATION FOR AN ORANGE GROVE.

SPECIAL reference should be had to drainage, soil, water protection, forest protection, proximity to fertilizers, and facilities for transportation. The soil for a grove should be thoroughly drained, either naturally or artificially. Not only should the surface water be carried off, but the drainage should be so deep as to allow roots, and especially the tap-root, to penetrate for several feet. Some think that less than ten feet is not sufficient. But there are in this State groves of fine old trees and good bearers with considerably less than ten feet of drained soil. The sour stock will flourish on a much wetter soil than the sweet. And it may be that these groves that have long done well in such localities are sour stocks budded. Where choice of location can be made, and especially if sweet stocks are to be planted, select a soil well drained by nature. Art and labor can accomplish a great deal, but it costs something, and the effect is not so permanent as when nature has done the work. If no positive evil arise from a wet subsoil in close proximity to the surface, still there are reasons why a deep, dry, or moist soil is better.

While it is true that the principal feeders of the orange lie near the surface, yet whoever will take the pains to examine the roots of an old orange tree grown in a deep and well-drained subsoil will find that these roots have penetrated for many feet deep into the earth and in all directions from the tree. Now if trees have been set twenty feet apart in the grove and the soil is drained but one foot deep, the roots of each tree have but four hundred cubic feet of soil in which to feed—$20 \times 20 = 400$. But if the soil has been drained to the depth of ten feet, then the feeding ground for the roots has been increased tenfold, and instead of four hundred cubic feet of soil in which to feed, the tree has four thousand cubic feet—$20 \times 20 \times 10 = 4000$. This advantage is more especially to be considered where the subsoil is sandy, as in such a soil air and other nutriment for the roots penetrate to a greater depth. But there are some of these wet soils found in our State that are positively poisonous to the orange, as they contain a large per centum of salt—*chloride of sodium.* Such is the case with soils underlaid with "hard-pan," a stratum seemingly of dark sandstone, underlying many sections of our State, and generally but a few feet from the surface. Analysis will probably show this "hard-pan" to be a concrete of sand, iron, and salt. The best surface indication of the presence of "hard-pan" is an abundance of saw palmetto with an abundance of roots above the surface. The palmetto feeds largely upon salt, its roots containing an unusually large per cent. But "what is fun" and life to the palmetto is death to the orange, as well as to the pockets of hundreds of those who have attempted in vain to grow oranges on lands underlaid with "hard-pan." If your land has on it an abundance of saw palmetto with roots on the surface, do not select that location for an orange grove until you have dug a few feet below the surface in search of "hard-pan." If you wish to ascertain the depth of natural drainage, revisit the hole twenty-four hours after it is dug, and measure the distance from the top of the water to the surface of the ground. The distance is the depth of the natural drainage of the soil.

The orange will grow in a variety of soils—in clayey, sandy, shelly, or loamy soils; in hammocks black or gray; on pine lands or black-jack ridges. It does well on soil underlaid with clay or sand. It will even do well on a light soil underlaid with white sand if fertilizers are annually applied. But whoever wishes to plant an orange grove should be careful to select the best available soil. Perhaps the poorest soil suitable for orange-growing is that underlaid with a white sand, as such a soil leaches very readily the soluble manure. Perhaps the best soil is found in our dark gray hammock with deep soil underlaid with a yellow clay or yellow sand subsoil. The natural growth should be tall and large, with an abundance of live oak and hickory, as such a growth would indicate an abundance of lime. Of our pine land, that on which the hickory is found mixed with the pine, with yellow subsoil, should rank first. Such a soil is really a mixed hammock and pine. Next to this is the pine mixed with willow, oak, and black-jack. Considering the ease with which such lands as the last two classes are cleared and planted, and the readiness with which the orange grows on them, they deserve a high rank, and especially if fertilizers are close at hand. In selecting a location in the purely pine lands, select that which is thickly set with tall trees, well drained, and with a yellow subsoil. Such soils, if occasionally dressed with alkaline manures, grow the orange admirably.

While with proper care the orange may be grown successfully in almost any portion of the State o Florida, still it is wise to select a location which may combine all conditions favorable to the best results. Among the favorable conditions we would mention water protection. Whoever has travelled over the State, not by railroad or steamboat, but through the country, and noted the effects of frost here and there upon the orange trees, and especially at the close of a severe winter, must attach great importance to water protection. Its advantages were known to the old settlers, as witness their frequent advice to those who in later years have gone into the orange business. Its advantages were known to and made available by nature so far back that " the memory of man knoweth not to the contrary," as witness the many wild-orange groves to the south-east of lakes and rivers. As our coldest winds come from the north-west, the benefit of water protection on any given location is in proportion to the width of the water lying to the north-west, and the proximity of such a body of water to said location. There may be seeming exceptions to this general rule. Air currents are governed by laws similar to those governing water. Hence, when any obstruction suddenly opposes a current, whether of air or water, an eddy or circular motion is given to the current. Bodies of timber with dense undergrowth standing on the north or north-west of a grove and along the shore of the river or lake have the effect of creating a rolling current of air like a breaker from the ocean rolling over a sandbar, and so, when the wind is from the north-west, bring down upon the grove a stratum of freezing air from above. The remedy for this is to clear out the underbrush along the shore and allow the warmer air from the surface of the water to flow through the grove. The taller trees should stand to keep the violence of the wind from the orange grove, and to check the violence of the air current upon the moist soil, which readily yields its moisture along with its heat to a strong air current, and so intensifies the cold. It is regretted that some good locations along the St. Johns have been marred, and groves made to suffer damage from want of attention to the above. The above facts also account for the well-known fact that the frost sometimes "strikes in spots or streaks."

Proximity to fertilizers is another favorable condition to be considered. The orange tree is a ravenous feeder and an abundant bearer, and however fertile the original soil may be, and even though it should be sufficient to produce fine trees and sustain them for a few years, any soil would finally become exhausted and need to be replenished. Commercial manures can be bought, but even when transportation is cheap the cost is considerable. The abundant and frequent deposits of muck in almost every locality have been shown by repeated experiments to be a valuable fertilizer. It would be well for the person looking for a location for an orange grove to have an eye to such a deposit close to the place for the intended grove. Leaves and ashes from a hammock close at hand, a shell bank, or limestone from which lime may be procured, should also be considered.

Facilities for transportation is the last item to be noticed in this chapter of favorable conditions to be considered in locating an orange grove. One other condition will be discussed in a separate chapter. The orange will bear transportation well, whether the expense of transportation or perishableness of the fruit be considered. But it would be well for the reader contemplating planting oranges to estimate the cost of hauling, say five miles by wagon or cart, an average crop of oranges grown on an acre, before he locates too far from a navigable stream or from a railroad. He can make the estimate for himself, and it will certainly have some weight in determining the location.

Some of the finest young trees I have seen in the State stand upon a sandy loam—the original growth pine—underlaid with clay four or five feet below the surface, on which rested a thin stratum of marl. I have seen trees six years from the seed on such soils produce from four hundred to five hundred oranges.

CHAPTER VIII.

THE ADVANTAGES OF PARTIAL FOREST SHELTER.

THE frequent discussion of the subject considered in this chapter among orange growers, its importance to all, and especially its importance to many portions of the State where success must ever depend upon either forest or some artificial protection, demands careful attention. Many persons have heretofore considered it unnecessary, and the idea even absurd. But years of experience and observation, and especially the experience of the winter of 1876-7, have made many converts. Let the reader consider some facts that may be mentioned.

Wild groves have grown luxuriantly, have borne abundantly, and lasted, no one knows how long, not suffering, so far as the writer has been informed, even from the severe frost of 1835; and all under forest protection. Again, all through Florida in almost every old settled community, and even in the southern tier of counties in Georgia, there are a few old trees standing and bearing well fine fruit. Hundreds seeing these trees have thought that what has been done once can be done again, and have planted in the immediate vicinity of such trees, but unfortunately in the open field, or, what is equally fatal, where the morning sun would smite the orange tree after a frost; and have failed. They have failed to consider that these trees that have survived so long and done so well were planted in almost a dense forest, when only a few forest trees had been cut to give place to the cabin of the early settler; or that they were planted on the north or west side of the house and thus never exposed to sudden thawing; that under some such protection of house or forest they passed through the tender age of their early life until their own boughs could furnish their trunks the protection needed. As to the questions of productiveness and thrift under partial forest protection, they are settled by the success of the few who in the face of opposing theories have planted and succeeded. Some of the most thrifty young groves in the State, grown with less expense and equal to any of their age in productiveness, have been grown under the shelter of the pine or oak trees. Many groves in a most flourishing condition, and supposed to be well located with reference to protection from frost, some far south and with considerable water to the north-west, were seriously damaged in the winter of 1876-7, and many trees beginning to bear entirely killed; but the writer has not heard of a single instance of damage to trees in that winter where they were protected by forest trees standing to the south and east of the oranges.

Even the lemon, in '76-7, much tenderer than

the orange, was unhurt where so protected. One other instance. On the south or south-east of Orange Lake stood two beautiful and extensive orange groves side by side. They were wild groves budded and just coming into bearing. They both had the same water protection. One grove was judiciously protected by forest trees left standing at suitable intervals; the other grove was without such forest protection. All the forest trees had been cut down. A few days after the severe frost of the winter of 1876-7 the sheltered grove was still as green as in midsummer, while the other appeared as though a fire had swept through it. Its leaves were dead or fallen, while thousands of dollars' worth of fruit, frozen and spoiled, hung upon the naked branches. The owner estimates that if he had left a few forest trees in his grove they would now be worth to him twenty thousand dollars. Are not such facts sufficient to check somewhat the reckless destruction of our noble forest trees and nature's chosen protectors?

In leaving trees for purposes of shelter for the orange, the direction given in Chapter III. on budding sour groves should be attended to. Suitable trees at suitable distances should be left. Three things are especially desirable : 1st, the rays of the early morning sun should be kept from falling directly on the frosted trees. As the sun hangs far to the south during our coldest weather, tall forest trees on the south and east would materially benefit orange trees standing from one to two hundred feet from them ; 2d, the rays of the sun should be permitted to fall, during some portion of the day, and in summer during a considerable portion of the day, upon each tree in the grove, as the rays of the sun, direct or indirect, are essential to plant life and health. But in our sunny climate and long summers, shade and sun alternating throughout the day are found to be most favorable to many plants ; 3d, the roots of the forest trees should be kept out of the way of the principal feeders of the orange. Of course the orange trees should be as thoroughly cultivated as if they stood in the open field. Failures in forest culture—and there have been some abominable failures — have occurred only where these points have been disregarded.

The following plan is suggested as one to which it is believed no reasonable exception can be made. Select a forest of tall and thickly set trees, whether of pine or hammock. Clear out the underbrush so as to allow a free circulation of air and to enable you to lay off more accurately your land. This done, lay off a straight line as the base of operating. Allowing your land to be a plat of five acres lying north and south, let this base line run east and west fifty feet north of and parallel to your southern boundary. Run a second line one hundred and five feet north of and parallel to the first ; so continue through the plat, running these east and west lines at intervals between, alternating from fifty to one hundred and five, and from one hundred and five to fifty feet apart. Now begin on the east side, and fifty feet from your eastern boundary you can run your base line perpendicular to your first base line. Go through the plat as before, alternating the distances between the lines from fifty to one hundred and five feet apart. You now have your land laid off in smaller squares of fifty feet, and parallelograms of fifty by one hundred and five feet. The timber on these smaller squares and parallelograms is to be left standing. You have also a number of large squares 105 x 105, or about one quarter of an acre each. These larger squares are to be cleared of the timber and made ready for planting orange trees, and each square will be found to be surrounded on all sides by a strip of timber fifty feet wide. Around these squares next to the timber cut a ditch two and a half, or, if you wish, three feet deep, so as to cut all the roots of forest trees that would interfere with the orange. To prevent this ditch from draining the moisture from the grove, fill it with the litter from the orange land and leaves from the forest. The next year clear out this ditch, use the rotten leaves as a fertilizer for your grove, and fill the ditch again with leaves from the forest around. By this means you can have an endless supply of manure close at hand, and you can have the benefit of the sun and the benefit of forest protection without any damage from the roots of the forest trees.

ADVANTAGES OF FOREST SHELTER. 59

In sections where the frost does not fall so heavily these squares for the orange may be greatly enlarged. But for the northern tier of counties in this State, where there may not be sufficient water protection, the dimensions given are large enough.

With such a system as the above no man in Florida who has the soil and the timber need hesitate to plant largely of this valuable fruit, both for himself and for market.

In the cut below, the dark lines represent the forest which has not been cut away ; the white spaces represent the spaces cleared for orange trees.

CHAPTER IX.

"THE FROST LINE" AND "THE ORANGE BELT."

MUCH has been said and written in certain portions of Florida concerning "the frost line" and "the orange belt." I regret to put into this treatise a single line that savors of controversy. But justice and truth demand that certain statements be corrected, and the public informed as to the facts. There are so many good places in Florida that many men who have places imagine theirs to be best. Now it is very fortunate that there are so many good places, but it is very unfortunate that one section should be praised by its inhabitants to the detriment of another equally good. No good has come to the State at large, and I doubt if any will come, in the long run, to the special community that pursues such an unjust course. The climate of Florida is so excellent, her soil so varied, her attractions so great, that multitudes will continue to come, as they are now coming, from the Northern and Western States, and from Europe, till all our goodly land is filled with a thrifty and contented population. Do not let any of her citizens say anything that would injure the adopted mother of us all.

As to "the frost line," there is no portion of the peninsula of Florida that is not subject to occasional frost. I have seen the effects of frost as low down as Fort Myers. Persons whose statements are entirely reliable, and residents of the section, have told me time and again that they have occasionally had their vegetables killed on the extreme southern capes of the peninsula. That frost is modified by latitude there is no question; that the southern portions of the State are less liable to frost than the northern portions there is no doubt; but do not deceive the immigrant by saying or implying that any portion of the mainland of Florida is entirely exempt from frost. And I do not know that this is to be deprecated. For while "Jack Frost" is an unskilled pruner, and by the little cutting he does in Florida may do some hurt, yet I think upon the whole both the orange tree and the health of the inhabitants are the better for his visits. I am sure my own orange trees were never so free from insects and in so healthy condition as to-day, eight months after the frost of December, 1880. And the only trees of my grove now giving indication of rust on the fruit are those where the frost left a few leaves, giving a wintering and start to the rust insect.

As to "the orange belt," there is no "orange belt" in Florida, unless those who so frequently use that expression mean to embrace the entire State. I do not mean to say that certain portions of the

State are not more favorable to the growth of the orange than other portions, but I do mean to say that the orange is so hardy that it can be grown profitably in any part of Florida where proper cultivation is bestowed and available protection given against the effects of frost. No finer oranges are grown than are grown in West Florida. On Fort George Island, at the mouth of the St. John's River, the thermometer fell to 16°, and yet the young grove of Mr. Stuart, planted according to the diagram given in the last chapter, is at present writing in fine condition. A few trees have done well on the mainland across the line dividing Florida and Georgia, while on the islands along the coast old groves in good condition are to be found as high up as South Carolina. The frost of last winter caused the leaves to drop from the trees of the last-named groves, but the owners with whom I have recently conferred report their trees in good condition.

I do not wish to be understood as advising persons who wish to come to Florida exclusively to plant oranges to settle in Middle Florida. Other portions of the State would suit better for this business. But were I owner of some of the fine lands of the above-named section, and had such excellent protection as their fine forests and lakes afford, I should not hesitate to plant largely of the golden fruit.

CHAPTER X.

THE EFFECT OF FROST ON PLANTS.

THIS is a matter of such moment that it needs to be closely studied, and, if possible, thoroughly understood by all persons engaged in agricultural or horticultural pursuits. Either extreme of heat or cold is damaging to vegetation. Some plants are hardier than others, and so are less easily affected by either extreme. Some families of plants are so hardy that they extend over nearly the habitable part of our globe. Some perennials are created with reference to greater heat, and are so limited in their natural condition to the tropics or the torrid zone. Others are created with reference to extreme cold, and hence are found in Arctic regions or on lofty mountains. While others, annuals, reach maturity within a few months, in order that their growth may be extended over a wider area of earth. These live in cold climates only during the warm months. Some plants are limited to a very narrow belt. Humboldt gives the natural limit of the orange from 12° to 40° north latitude. Of course the orange can survive in this higher latitude only where the climate is affected by warm ocean currents.

Cold and heat are nature's great agents in breaking down rocks, disintegrating earths, and so converting into soluble manures for the use of plants what otherwise would be useless for plant-life. In higher latitudes the effect of cold is to suspend circulation during the winter months, in order that the soil may store up during winter an ample amount of plant-food for the great effort of Nature to make fruit. It is owing to this that vegetation in cold regions puts forth more rapidly during the short summers, and that fruit trees in such regions are so uniform in the production of fruit. This hint should be taken by the growers of oranges in the semi-tropics. When their trees fail to put on a sufficient quantity of fruit, let them manure in the fall or early winter—sufficiently soon for the manure to reach the roots before the buds begin to swell. Thus stimulated, the bush that would only put forth the less effort and produce a leaf or branch may be forced to the greater effort to produce fruit. This fall manuring might prove injurious to a young tree, with wood too immature for the production of fruit, by forcing it to put forth shoots so early as to be nipped by a late frost. But it would have the opposite effect on a bearing tree, by forcing the production of blossom and fruit instead of tender branches, as both blossom and fruit of the orange will stand much more cold than the newly started leaves and branches. I have not infrequently seen considerable frost fall upon both blossom and young fruit without any damage. In regions where there is no frost, the orange tree, when sufficiently fed, is in the habit of fruiting continuously.

When water freezes it expands. It is owing to this law that cold is so fatal to plants fully charged with sap, mainly composed of water. The sap, by expanding, ruptures the cellular tissue—the woody cells containing the sap. The oxygen of the atmosphere penetrates these ruptures, and, combining with the sap, induces fermentation. Unless prevented, either by artificial or natural means, this fermentation will extend itself to contiguous parts until the whole plant is destroyed, when only a small portion of the tender wood may, in the first instance, have been frosted. Nature's method is to close behind the rupture all avenues against the penetration of the atmosphere by a deposit of glutinous or gummy substance furnished by the inner bark. When the old wood or bark decays or drops off, this inner becomes the outer bark, and so the damage is greatly and sometimes wholly repaired. The artificial remedy is to cut off the frosted wood and at once apply an artificial skin impervious to the atmosphere. Many persons who have treated frosted orange and lemon trees have failed at this latter point. They have cut off a part or all the frosted wood, but left a surface to be cracked by the sun or drying of the wood, and so only opened fresh avenues for the penetration of the atmosphere.

It is better not to cut at all unless the wound is to be covered at once. Shellac dissolved in alcohol, or a coating of whitewash, or a soft paste made of lime and fresh cow-dung, are good applications. When a plant is frosted, the direct rays of the sun will suddenly thaw and so contract the bark as to enlarge the avenues to the atmosphere and make the cold more fatal in effect. Hence, shading a frozen plant, or thoroughly drenching with water, is often a preventive of injury. I have seen orange trees saved by setting a pine bough or other shelter on the south and east, and when the thaw occurs in the afternoon, on the west side of the tree.

It has before been mentioned that the sowing of oats thickly upon the ground in the fall will check the circulation of sap during winter by taking up the soluble manures. Nature has two methods of fortifying perennials against the effects of severe frost. One method is to deplete the tree of sap during winter. Deciduous trees are so rendered hardy. Their wood during winter contains so little sap that the expansion by frost is not sufficient to rupture the cells. Another method is to so commingle oil with the water of the sap as to counteract this law of expansion universal to frozen water. While frozen water expands, frozen oil or hydrocarbonates contract. The clockmaker has faintly imitated nature in this. By combining different metals in the rod which suspends the pendulum he has made the law of expansion furnish him with a rod equal in length whatever the changes from heat to cold. All resinous woods, such as the pine, the fir, etc., are of the class so protected by nature. Hence, though found in almost all habitable latitudes, these are under no necessity of shedding their foliage.

The orange tree approximates in the character of its sap to this order of plants, and is therefore, though a tropical plant, able to stand the changes of a semi-tropical climate.

CHAPTER XI.

TRANSPLANTING.

BEFORE the work of transplanting begins, the soil for the grove should be well prepared. It is most generally the case that the great hurry to get the trees into the ground causes much neglect at this point, but this policy is a bad one. The haste should have reference to the early fruiting and rapid growth of the tree; and they are not brought about by careless preparation of the soil. The soil should be deeply and thoroughly broken, and the ground cleared of the roots. To insure the setting of the trees a proper and uniform depth, the ground should be levelled with harrow or drag. No manure should be used at the time of setting, nor before, unless applied some months before setting and thoroughly incorporated with the soil.

The best time for setting trees is the late winter or early spring, before the new wood has started. The ground is then cool, and the roots in as dormant condition as at any time during the year. It is better that the ground should be wet and the setting followed by showers. But wet soil is not so essential at this time of the year as it is when the transplanting has been done later and the ground and sun are warmer. If the work of transplanting has not been completed before the warm, dry weather of spring has set in and before new wood has advanced far, it is best to defer the work till the frequent showers of August and September begin to fall. Good results sometimes follow summer, fall, and winter planting, but these seasons are not so good as the months of February, March, and April. One exception to this rule should be stated. Where trees are to be set under forest protection so that they will escape any damage from frost, the late fall is the best time, as trees set at that time are well established and ready to start by the spring.

In taking up the trees great care should be taken to prevent breaking or bruising the roots. As many roots as possible should be taken up. If the distance from the nursery to the site of the grove be short, and the nursery rows have been well manured with muck, and the ground is wet at the time of lifting the trees from the nursery, much of the soil can be taken along with the roots. Immediately on lifting the roots from the ground they should be trimmed with a sharp knife wherever they are found to have been bruised or broken. The lower part of the tap-root also should be cut off to prevent its doubling up on being reset. Twelve or eighteen inches is sufficiently long for the tap-root. Put the tree under shade, and cover the roots with wet moss as soon as possible. Do not allow the fibrous roots to dry, as they are very delicate and soon perish. Should they die before setting, cut them off, for if left on after they have died they will only impede the starting of new rootlets. Keep them protected up to the moment of setting, taking but one tree at a time from its covering of moss. To insure still further against damage to the tender roots, have on hand a half barrel of muck made into a thin paste, and as fast as the trees are lifted and the roots trimmed, plunge the roots into this paste, take them out, and wrap in moss.

The holes for the trees should be freshly dug. The work of setting is easily and rapidly done by three hands working together—one to dig the holes, one to prune and set the tree, and a third to fill in. The holes should be dug in the shape of an inverted saucer or truncated cone with about two inches of the top cut off. Proceed thus: Around the stake which marks the place for the tap-root, with a shovel or hoe take away the soil, letting the tool strike the top of the soil at the stake, and continue to dig deeper into the soil until at a distance of eighteen inches from the stake it has penetrated six inches below the surface. Proceed thus around the stake until it is completed. This gives the greatest depth of the hole on the outer edge or perimeter of the circle. Now take up the stake, and cut two inches of the top off the cone. Where the stake stood, push down the spade by working it back and forth until it has penetrated the ground about eighteen inches, or the full length of the tap-root of the tree to be set. Now insert the tap-root in this hole made by the spade. Be careful not to set the tree deeper than it grew in the nursery. With the hand pack the soil firmly around the tap-root. Next spread the lateral roots over the cone, taking care to distribute them evenly over the cone. Throw on two inches of dirt and press it firmly with the feet. Finish by throwing in soil and levelling the ground, leaving the last layer of soil untrod.

Before the tree is left it should be trimmed with shears in proportion to the trimming done to the roots.

If planting is done in summer or in hot weather, and the ground is not protected by forest trees, it is better to mulch.

If trees are older than three years, and wild grown, it may be necessary to dig the holes deeper than directed above, but the point of this caution is against deep setting. The writer is satisfied that more trees have been diseased and retarded in their growth, and frequently killed, by deep setting than by any other one cause.

CHAPTER XII.

THE DISTANCE APART.

IN the grove the distance apart at which trees should be placed depends upon the character of the trees to be set. The seedling should have the greatest distance, the sweet seedling budded less, and the sour stock budded least of all.

In Europe, where budding on sour stock is generally practised, and land is much costlier than in this country, trees are set much closer than is the custom in Florida. In the former country, where set in the open ground, they are frequently put as close as ten or twelve feet apart, and where artificial covering during the winter is resorted to, still nearer. But in Europe orange trees never grow to the size they attain in Florida. In some of the old groves in this State where the trees stand forty feet apart the ground is completely covered by the branches of trees that have grown up since 1835. Thirty or forty years, however, is too long a time to leave the land uncovered. Trees planted nearer together will soon protect each other.

The rule I have observed for some time is to set budded trees on sour stock 21 x 21 feet; budded trees on sweet stock, 25 x 25, and sweet seedlings, 30 x 30 feet.

When the planter wishes to set the budded and seedling in the same grove, a good plan is to set the sweet seedling 30 x 30, and then in the centre of the square formed by four trees set a budded tree. The budded trees will come into bearing some years before the seedling trees, and by so much lessen the dead expense of the grove. Another advantage of the last-named plan is, that space will be economized and the trees still be at a uniform distance from each other.

CHAPTER XIII.

CULTIVATION.

THE orange will live with almost no cultivation, but it will only be a sickly existence. I know no plant, shrub, or tree that will pay better for good cultivation; none that will respond so certainly to thorough cultivation.

The ground in the grove should be kept level, the surface light. As far as the roots have extended the surface should not be stirred deeper than three inches. The more frequently it is stirred the better. Beyond the reach of the roots it is well to cultivate deep and frequently, but as the roots extend themselves this area of deep cultivation should be lessened. After the roots have extended themselves well over the ground, the best plow to be used is the sweep. A single thirty-two-inch sweep, or a gang plow, the middle or front plow twenty-two inches wide, and the two side plows fourteen inches each, does excellent work. It is better than the turning plow or cultivator. The sweep is much more uniform in the depth of its cutting than either. It is much more rapid in its work than the single plow. It is more apt to cut off the weeds below the surface and destroy them than the cultivator.

With such an implement, a grove free from stumps and litter is easily and cheaply kept in fine condition.

While the orange trees are young it is of advantage to keep the ground planted in garden crops—peas, beans, potatoes, tomatoes, anything that requires frequent work and will mature within a few weeks, partially shading the ground. Of course nothing should be taken from the ground without making adequate return in the form of manures. Suitable fertilizers will be noticed in a separate chapter.

Where the trees are planted far apart, and ten or twelve years will elapse before the ground will be all occupied by the orange, grapes and peaches will do well and prove profitable, provided the soil is well drained.

At no time should the roots of grass and weeds be allowed to mat themselves on land growing the orange. Not only will they draw heavily upon the soil while they are growing, but when turned over the turf and matted roots will necessarily leave the surface very irregular, causing the ground to dry rapidly under the influence of sun and wind. Some have advised cultivation to cease during August and September, alleging it to be better to allow the weeds and grass to grow after these months in order to check the fall growth, and thus allow the wood of the orange to so harden as to resist the influence of frost during the winter. But the writer has experimented extensively and *expensively*—considering results—with the above policy, and where others were pursuing the same policy he has advised them to try clean culture or garden crops on a part of the grove, and in every instance where the land has been kept thoroughly cultivated the trees have doubled, in size and thrift, those allowed to be left to the mercy of the weeds and grass.

Another result should be considered in this connection. Where grass and weeds are allowed to grow in the grove they are generally killed by the frost during the fall or winter. In this condition they absorb and part with moisture very readily, absorbing moisture when the atmosphere is warmer than the ground, and yielding it up when the atmosphere is cooler than the ground or the wind is blowing. But to part with moisture is to part with heat and increase the cold. In some sections of Europe, before the invention of ice machines, considerable ice was collected and stored away where the general temperature was only 40°. The freezing was induced by simply covering over lightly and surrounding the ice ponds with wet straw. The wind passing through the wet straw took up from the exposed and larger surface of the straw its moisture together with its heat and left the water to freeze. To leave any dry straw, weeds, or litter on the ground during the winter only intensifies the cold and invites the frost. The writer knows of several beautiful groves that were entirely frozen down from this cause, while others in the immediate vicinity were unhurt. Mulching during the winter has a similar effect. In this immediate neighborhood an old and beautiful orange tree was heavily mulched during winter. It was the only tree hurt by the frost in the grove that was hurt very badly, taking two or three years to recover. While the trees are young, keep the grove clear of grass and weeds, summer and winter. If you mulch during the summer, bury the mulching as the winter approaches ; dig holes and bury the litter. This instruction is for young and tender trees. When the surface of the ground is well shaded by older trees, general mulching is recommended, as will be seen in another chapter.

In cultivating the grove with the plow there is a constant tendency of the soil to pile up around the trunk of the tree. This should be watched, and if the crown of the lateral surface roots is a half inch below the surface, from this or from deep planting, the soil should be drawn from around the trunk till the upper sides of these roots are brought to the top of the ground. If the upper parts of these roots are left bare for one or two inches, where trees are five or six years old, and for a greater distance where the trees are older, these roots develop very rapidly, and not only furnish stout braces to the trunk, but great arteries for conveying life and food from the soil. This point is so little understood and attended to by many cultivators that it may be well to explain further. This development of the crown roots is nature's plan when it is not interfered with. Whoever will visit and examine a natural forest, whether of orange or other trees, will find the top of the crown roots from one to several inches above the ground and running in many instances, as great braces, well up the trunk of the tree. This development of the crown is slow at first, but increases in proportion as the upper surface of the roots lift themselves above the surface of the ground. This development can be hastened by taking away the earth from above the roots for a short distance from the tree, as mentioned above. The principle is the same as that adopted for the development of the bulb of the onion by taking the earth from around it. The root of the plant, being more porous than the stem, parts more readily with its moisture at the point where it is exposed, and hence the thickened sap lodges more readily at that point, and so hardens into wood and increases the growth. As the upward circulation passes only through the new or sap wood, this enlarged base furnishes, at the very seat of life and strength, new and increased capacity to the tree.

CHAPTER XIV.

THOROUGH CULTIVATION.

WHEN the preceding chapter was published, four years ago, the writer hoped he had put the importance of good cultivation so forcibly as to induce any reader of the first edition of this treatise to fairly cultivate any orange trees that he might plant with the wish to make them productive and profitable. But four years of additional observation and experience convince the writer that a large percentage of those who are engaged in orange-planting in Florida are wasting time and means by careless cultivation. Now let me drop this indirect manner of speaking of the writer as the third person. I want to look you in the eye, reader, and say to you if you do not intend to cultivate your trees thoroughly, or have them cultivated thoroughly, do not waste money by buying land and having it planted in trees. In no business is the old aphorism truer than in orange-growing, "What is worth doing at all is worth doing well." I would add, what is poorly done in this business is apt to bring poor return or no return to the owner of a grove. I will give one or two instances of many, very many, that have come under my observation.

A little more than twelve months ago a gentleman from Middle Florida purchased a portion of a grove that had been planted two or three years in Orange County. At the time of the purchase I could see no advantage in size or thrift of trees or excellence of soil in favor of that portion of the grove retained over that portion sold. Since the division of the grove the purchaser has had his part of the grove plowed once or twice. The other part of the grove has been well cultivated and fertilized. To-day the cultivated trees look as though they were several years older than the uncultivated—this difference thus brought about in one year. One other instance: Some years ago a neighbor bought several hundred trees from a nurseryman, who advised him to suspend cultivation in August, in order that the growth of grass and weeds might check the growth of fall wood as a prevention of frost. Another party advised the planter to cultivate one half his trees throughout the summer and note the different results. He did so, cultivating small crops among the trees. The advantage gained in half a year is so marked that four years, so far from obliterating the evidence, has made it only the more apparent.

One word about this often-expressed opinion and advice, "to stop cultivation in August, in order to check the fall growth and give the wood time to harden before frost." The orange tree, if well cultivated, will make from three to four growths during summer. If not manured later than June, thorough cultivation will only hasten forward the seasons of growth and ripening of the wood before fall. Besides, vigorous health with well-ripened wood is one of the best protections against damage by frost. If the object be to prevent any winter growth and suspend active circulation of sap during winter, this can be better secured by seeding the land heavily in oats. The growing oats will take up all soluble manures in the soil and leave the young orange trees to rest till spring.

Various discussions have been entered into throughout the State as to the relative value of deep and shallow culture. The disputants on the different sides have usually reached their conclusions not by generalizing, but by "induction" from a single experience or observation. One gentleman who had met with marked success in orange-growing wrote as the secret of success, "Deep plowing," "Tear up the roots." Convinced that there must be something unusual about the soil that would produce fine trees and fruit under such a method, I visited his grove, found it planted upon an oak scrub with no fertility in the upper soil, but underlaid a few feet from the surface with clay, on which rested a stratum of marl. The mystery was solved. There being no nourishment in the upper soil, the roots had gone down to where they might find food, and so were little disturbed by the deep plowing. Indeed, the deep plowing only let in the sunlight and air for the further penetration of roots. But this case is exceptional. Nature's method is to deposit the most valuable manures near the surface of the ground. Trees, weeds, and grasses are, by means of roots, reaching down to bring up some of these manures from beneath, while the leaves are reaching out to gather other manures from the atmosphere, and so from these two directions nature is gathering and combining in organized and useful forms substance for plant-food to be deposited upon the surface of the soil, to be carried down by means of rain to the roots of the growing crops. Hence with nearly all plants, and especially those having yellow roots, the orange included, the most abundant feeders lie near the surface. Hence the most natural means of cultivating a grove is to mulch the entire surface with sufficient material to prevent any growth of weeds or grass. This method gives a treble advantage—it secures sufficient moisture for the roots of the orange, it avoids the necessity of cultivation with either hoe or plow, and gives sufficient fertility to the soil. This method is especially adapted to natural groves that have been budded and to groves planted on low lands. In the first instance, nature has already placed the roots near the surface, and it is poor policy to disturb the roots by plow or hoe, and so attempt to force nature from its long-established habit. In the second instance the roots will not penetrate a wet soil, but grow near the surface. The flourishing condition of the groves at Federal Point, on the St. John's, and other groves where the surface water can be carried off by shallow ditches, sufficiently demonstrates that the orange can be successfully grown on low lands by mulching, or by shallow cultivation with the hoe, or, as in some instances where the soil is rich, by mowing the grass and weeds twice a year and leaving them to rot on the ground.

Where material is abundant and near at hand, mulching is the cheapest method of cultivation, as it is equivalent to both manure and frequent disturbing the surface with hoe and plow. In many parts of Florida abundant material is at hand. Leaves from our forests can easily be collected and carted to the ground. In many places a horse-rake can be used for gathering them in piles. The wire-grass can be cut by hoe, or better, where the forest is open, by means of a mower and horse-rake. Our marsh lands along our extended coast and the banks of our numerous rivers and lakes in Florida are at no distant day to be utilized and made valuable by furnishing thousands of tons annually for the purpose of mulching. The first year of my residence in Florida, living on a lake with a margin covered with grass growing above the water, I constructed a flat-bottom boat with a mower attached in front and driven by man-power, which enabled three men working a half day in a week to furnish nine head of horses with abundant and nutritious forage.

Such a machine impelled by steam could be made to do the work of a hundred men, and furnish mulching to growers on the banks of our rivers at a cost not exceeding one or two dollars per ton.

CHAPTER XV.

PRUNING.

PRUNING is universally adopted by nature. In the forest all the branches of the little oaks and pines are near the ground. But as the trees grow these lower branches die and drop off. A few years later we behold thousands of graceful, well-trimmed trunks. Where the oak grows up in the open field its method is to prune the inner branches and extend the surface, giving what fruit-growers call an open head. The grape-vine prunes itself. Where its branches are thickest the tendrils first strangle and then cut off some of the excessive branches. It is the Divine plan. "I am the true vine, and my Father is the husbandman. Every branch in me that beareth not fruit, he cutteth away; and every branch that beareth fruit, he pruneth it that it may bear more fruit." Wise is the man who will follow such teaching. Happy is the man who has a taste for such work and can take up the vocation first taught man when "the Lord God put him into the garden of Eden to dress it and to keep it;" especially where he can dress a garden of this golden fruit—a relic of Eden—that is "pleasant to the sight and good for food."

It may be said, "If nature prunes at all, let her do it all." Yes, and it may be said, "If nature plants and grows the corn at all, why should I take the trouble to plant and cultivate?" But such a man will reap little more than the harvest of his folly and indolence. Nature makes suggestions, but does not propose to do all the work where man's interest is especially concerned. Even before thorns and briers had sprung up, it was man's duty and to his interest to "dress the garden" so perfectly planted. Again, where nature prunes, knots and dead wood often become the starting points for extensive decay. But where a living branch is cut off with a sharp knife from a vigorous tree, the wound soon heals over, leaving no scar nor injury.

The writer has practised on a grove of about 4000 trees all the methods of pruning, and not pruning, to satisfy himself as to the best method. Nor has he spared himself the trouble of visiting many of the best groves in the State, watching the operations of others, and questioning them closely as to their practice and the results. He will not trouble the reader with the many theories advanced, much less with discussing them. A few essential points are all that are necessary to be attended to.

In pruning, the sharper the knife or saw, the better. Let the cut be clean and smooth. When the knife is used it is better to cut *up* than down, as the downward cut is apt to split the wood and peel off the bark. Do the principal pruning in the spring. By all means avoid fall or winter pruning, as it is apt to start new wood at a time when it is most exposed to damage from frost. Cut off all dead wood, and up to or a little into the living wood. Thereby the wound heals more readily. As a general rule cut off all diseased branches, especially if they have become so far diseased as to fail to develop healthy leaves. Do not trim up the trunk too high. Encourage the lower branches to extend themselves well around the trunk and far over the surface of the ground. If they do not touch the ground they are not too low. As the tree grows these branches will continue to droop nearer the ground until the lowest may have to be cut off after a while ; but this late cutting off is much better than to have the trunk exposed either to sun or cold.

Give and keep an open head to the tree. To do this, select the most vigorous lateral branches, leaving some on all sides of the tree, so as to obtain a head as uniformly balanced as possible. After cutting off the other branches close to the trunk, trim up these selected branches almost to a point, leaving only a few of the terminal smaller branches. When this is done the tree will look like a skeleton, and you will likely conclude you have used the knife too freely. But if this pruning has been done in the spring, and you keep the " water" shoots pulled off the trunk, and cultivate well, you will find the trunk by winter inclosed in a beautiful head, with a dense wall of foliage on the outside. The next spring trim these laterals in a similar manner, allowing the first laterals to rebranch a little distance from the trunk so as to be able to fill up the larger area by fall. Continue this method till your tree is large enough to bear its first crop. You can then slacken your pruning so as to encourage the fruiting.

There are several advantages arising from judicious pruning. Whenever a branch dies, it not only ceases to benefit the tree, but becomes a drain on its sap and vitality, as an ulcer to the human body. The same is true, to some extent, with a diseased branch. Moreover, as a branch begins to die, its fermenting sap is slowly taken up into the general circulation, and so the disease extends itself sometimes to the entire tree, unless it be cut off below the sound wood. This is especially the case when the frost has partially killed the young wood. The writer has known quite vigorous trees to be killed, not only to the ground, but entirely, by neglect at this point. The open head not only gives room for the free circulation of air through the branches, but also enables the gardener to watch the trunk and larger branches and remove from them insects that might prove damaging. Another advantage, arising from the open head is, it causes the lower branches to extend themselves far out from the trunk, and so gives a greater bearing capacity to the tree. Trees in the grove of the writer pruned after this plan have doubled in development within two years, in their surface area, others standing by their side with the same treatment, except that the latter were not pruned.

CHAPTER XVI.

FERTILIZING.

THIS has never been sufficiently appreciated in the South. Her broad acres have always tempted to planting too much land and using too little manure. Somehow, when Northern men come South they, too, yield to the temptation and fall into the Southern fashion. And yet no soil responds more readily to the influence of manure than our warm Southern soil. The manure put by Peter Henderson on a single acre would be deemed by any Southern farmer ample for the broad fields of cotton stretching around his decaying mansion. A few men are wiser; they have ceased to fell the forest for more land, and are contracting the planted area of the old land. They are endeavoring to increase their crops by manuring. Such men have succeeded, and are still succeeding. Some I know have grown rich by such a policy.

No crop feeds more ravenously than the orange, and none will convert so large an amount of suitable fertilizers into fruit so profitably. Much of our Florida land will produce and sustain fine trees for a few years without the aid of manure; but after some years of fruiting the leaves will begin to turn yellow, indicating a deficiency in the soil. Some of our lands considered poorest—black-jack ridges—in the vicinity of dwellings grow fine trees, and continue to sustain fine crops of excellent oranges. But these trees so located are almost daily replenished with accidental deposits of nitrogenous manures (the principal fertilizers needed on black-jack lands), as well as considerable wood-ashes and soot from the daily fires of the kitchen, and suds from the washtub. The flourishing condition of these trees only shows the advantage of manures.

It is not safe to manure trees at the time of planting. In some instances this has succeeded very well, but only when the manure has been long composted and frequently turned, so that no fermentation will occur around the wounded roots. When manuring *will* be done thus early it is better to scatter it on the ground and turn it several times in the soil some weeks before the tree is planted.

After the tree has been planted and once started to grow, it is then well to manure it heavily till it begins to bear. Begin with a moderate quantity, applying near the outer extremity of the lateral roots, and increase the quantity every year and enlarge the area to which it is applied. When garden crops are planted, scatter the manure broadcast. Aim to make the ground rich—rich as a city garden. It will pay for the manure and cultivation if the ground be planted and well cultivated in crops, and especially if planted in vegetables where a market can be readily reached. There are several advantages derived from generous manuring when the trees are young : not only is the development of the tree hastened, but the tree is less liable to be attacked by some of the insects, and when attacked is better enabled to resist their ravages ; and when in vigorous health, but not making new wood during winter, it is less liable to be damaged by the influence of frost. To prevent this last-named evil the young tree should never be stimulated in the fall or latter part of the summer. It is much better to manure in the spring. Another advantage to be noted is, when trees are pushed before coming into bearing, the heavy manuring does no damage to the fruit.

The kind of fertilizer to be used depends largely upon the character of the soil. If the land planted was originally heavily set in hard wood, and the ashes of the wood, cut in clearing, have been scattered on the ground, it is more than likely that the soil for a few years will have a sufficiency of lime, soda, and potash. In that case nitrogenous manures will be needed. But if all the hard wood has been taken off the land and no ashes left, such a soil will likely have become poor in calcareous manures (as the readiness with which the pine springs up in our worn hammock lands shows), and should be treated as the pine lands, and manures applied containing all the elements of vegetable life used by the roots.

FERTILIZING.

Some of the commercial manures are valuable, when used in combination with other things, but none of them contain in the right proportions all the elements needed for the orange. The writer has used and seen used a large variety of these fertilizers, and some benefit has been derived from most of them. From others no advantage has been discoverable. A good article of ground bone, where the oils and phosphoric acid have not been too generally expelled by burning; Peruvian guano, and potash, both the nitrate and sulphate, are very good when combined with muck. These are especially valuable when early vegetables are to be grown among the orange trees, as they highly stimulate the soil and hasten forward both the vegetables and orange trees.

Land plaster should be especially mentioned as beneficial to our sandy soil, as it not only furnishes an important element to the soil, but in the absence of clay in most of our soil furnishes a valuable absorber and retainer of the volatile manures so easily expelled by our abundance of sunshine. The writer thinks he has seen another advantage in the use of land plaster in the check which the sulphur, contained in the plaster, has upon some of the insects which damage the trees.

Green crops turned under are highly beneficial to young trees. Rye, oats, and barley, sown in the fall and turned under in the spring and followed by one or two crops of cow peas during the summer, help forward a grove of trees wonderfully. It is still better if this be accompanied by a liberal dressing of wood-ashes. One ton to the acre is not too much.

Manures from the stables, cow-pens, hennery, and pig-sty, indeed from every place where waste is deposited, should first be deodorized by the liberal use of land plaster or sulphate of iron—copperas—dissolved in water and composted with muck, and be carefully saved and utilized. As they are highly stimulating, they should be composted with three or four times the quantity of muck, and frequently turned before using.

But of all the manures, that which is cheapest and most abundant is the muck to be found in our rivers, creeks, lakes, and ponds. A good article of muck is little less than decomposed vegetable matter. Leaves, wood, weeds, and grass, as they have fallen, have been washed into these deposits and decomposed under water so slowly and so excluded from the atmosphere that they have lost little of their original elements. Here they have been preserved by nature, as in the crucible of the chemist, for ages, and now lie in rich and vast deposits for the use of the orange-grower. Some who have supposed they were using muck have been mistaken. They have found a black sand with a little vegetable matter with it. If they had taken a little of it and washed it they would have found little else than sand, and some of it, that of a brown granular appearance, of a similar nature to "hard-pan." Such a deposit is of no value, and that containing the brown sand is actually injurious to the orange. Some who have used this kind of material have failed to discover any benefit and have cried out against all muck. But the time has passed for this. Too many have used muck and found it valuable for its merits to remain longer unknown. Where this deposit is close to the grove, an economical way to use it is to haul it at once from the bed and spread it broadcast over the ground and plow it in. It should not be allowed to dry in the sun, as it then becomes lumpy. If turned under the surface it soon incorporates itself with the soil. After it is applied and turned under, a top-dressing of ashes or lime would prove beneficial. If the deposit is some distance from the grove it is more economical to throw it into heaps near the bed, but under the shade, and still better to add a little lime slaked with salt water or ashes, as it is thrown in uniform layers. The pile soon heats and dries out, leaving the muck as friable as a bed of sand. It is then very light and easily handled and carted. In this condition it can be used in almost any quantities; the only danger to be feared from excessive use is in piling it up so deep over the roots as to smother them for a while. And yet if the crown roots are kept uncovered the surface roots soon find their way to the muck near the surface. The writer has had the orange roots penetrate, for several inches above the general surface, a pile of muck left for a few weeks near a tree.

Before trees reach the bearing state they should be fed with nitrogenous manures, but after they have begun to bear, potash and kindred manures should be liberally used. Nitrogenous manures encourage the development of new wood and foliage, while phosphate of lime and potash are necessary to an abundance of fruit. The yellow leaves of the tree indicate a deficiency of nitrogenous manures, while the dark green leaves show an abundance.

Where trees are slow in coming into bearing, or where old trees do not set sufficient fruit, give the trees a liberal manuring sufficiently early in the season to enable the rains to carry the soluble manure to the roots before the time of forming the button for the bloom. By so doing you develop the bud, that would otherwise only make foliage, into a fruit bud. It requires more nutriment to make fruit than wood, and hence the importance of this instruction.

In colder latitudes the frosts of winter lock up the circulation of fruit trees that nature may have sufficient time to store food for the greater effort to bear fruit. But in the milder climate of the orange regions this circulation is not always checked sufficiently to prevent the consumption of the soluble manures in the soil. And hence when the time of fruiting comes, there is not a sufficient supply of fertility in the soil to make the blossoms set the fruit, and so the tree makes the easier effort to form wood instead of fruit. After growth has been for a while suspended, by drought or poverty of soil, I have brought trees into blooming and bearing during midsummer by a liberal application of soluble manure. I have seen a grove that had previously borne only a few scattering oranges brought into liberal bearing by the application of a good dressing of manure in November.

Once more before leaving this subject : While commercial manures, properly combined and sufficiently concentrated, are a great convenience, owing to the ease with which they are distributed, the temptation to adulterate with something worthless, and sometimes something injurious to the orange, is so great that there is much uncertainty as to their real value. I have occasionally used manures of the same brand and from the same establishment which differed so greatly in their real value that while I have found one lot entirely satisfactory, another lot has proven quite worthless. The intelligent orange-grower can proceed with much more certainty if he can make his own manures. For this purpose no country can furnish better facilities than Florida. In addition to the abundance of material for mulching, already mentioned, there is such a vast quantity of muck, leaves, and grass from forests and marshes that with a few cattle or horses a large amount of valuable manure can be secured by those who are willing to take the trouble. Some of our planters in the State have made by this method as much as one ton of good manure per head of cattle or horses per month. And nothing is better for the orange than this well-rotted barnyard manure. If it is not convenient to keep stock, a good compost can be made by adding 300 pounds of ground bone and 200 pounds of muriate of potash to one cord of muck. Turn frequently the compost, and when well rotted apply broadcast at the rate of 1000 pounds per acre, and harrow.

CHAPTER XVII.

SPECIES, VARIETIES, ETC.

HITHERTO no mention has been made of any of the Citrus family except the sweet orange and the wild or sour orange—bigarade.

The methods of propagation and cultivation of all the family are so similar that no difference need be mentioned, except the fact that the citron, the lime, and the lemon, are much more tender than the orange, and need to be planted in more sheltered places.

Gallesio recognizes but four distinct species in the family: the orange (sweet), the bigarade (sour orange), the citron, and the lemon.

He justly remarks as to the varieties: "The citrus is a genus whose species are greatly disposed to blend together, and whose flower shows great facility for receiving extraordinary fecundation; it hence offers an infinite number of different races which ornament our gardens, and whose vague and indefinite names fill the catalogues." Gray remarks: "The species or varieties are much confused and mixed." Reese in his quotations from authorities makes a similar confession. But if the species and varieties are so confused in Europe, where the classification of the citrus family has been principally discussed, and where the multiplication of varieties has been somewhat held in check by their method of propagating the orange, mainly by graft or bud, what must be " the number of different races" which are to be found in Florida, where the general method of propagating the orange is from seed?

At the late meeting of our State Fruit Growers' Association a committee was charged with the work of naming our best marked varieties. They made a short report on the few varieties which came under their observation. But their work is not complete, nor likely to be for the next year or two. They are competent men, but their task is endless as well as important. Almost every community where the orange has been long grown from seed has some excellent and well-marked variety. Some of these varieties differ greatly. Some ripen early and others late. Some have thick tough skins with finely flavored fruit, and are well adapted to shipping a long distance, while others are of such a delicate skin and pulp that they will have to be eaten nearer home. Some are large and light bearers, while others are small and heavy bearers.

Many varieties differ greatly in color, from the pale orange to a reddish orange, and even to blood color. It would be well for those who intend planting budded trees, or propose to bud trees now growing, to select the most excellent kinds, whether they have yet been honored with a name or not, as it is the *quality* of the fruit and not the name which is needed. The name and classification will come in time. Any new and remarkably good varieties ought also to be brought to the notice of the above-named State committee on nomenclature. These gentlemen will do their duty, and Florida will be compelled to have her own nomenclature, as she has her own varieties.

The orange of Portugal and the China orange are two well-known varieties in Europe, and are frequently seen in Florida, but have changed somewhat by having been reproduced from seed.

The Orange of Portugal, or common sweet orange, is a tree growing to a great height when raised from seed. Its leaf is green, having a winged petiole; its shoots are whitish, its flowers entirely white and very odorous, though not equal in perfume to those of the bigarade.

Its fruit, ordinarily round, is sometimes flattened, sometimes a little oblong. The rind, less than an eighth of an inch in thickness, is of a reddish yellow, and full of aroma; the inner skin is a sallow white, spongy, and light. The sections, nine to eleven in number, contain a sweet juice, very refreshing and agreeable; its seeds are white and oblong, germinating very easily and reproducing usually the species with little change. There is a variety with no thorns; it is the race cultivated mostly by grafting, and is seen in all countries where this method of propagation is followed. In places where the orange is grown from seed it is rare to find it deprived of thorns.

The China Orange is a variety excelling all others in the perfection of its fruit, of which the juice is the sweetest, the most abundant, and the most perfumed. The skin is always smooth, glossy, and so thin that one can scarcely detach it from the pulp. This is characteristic of this variety.

The Red-fruited Orange is a singular variety. Its appearance, its leaf, its flower, are all exactly like the common orange. Its fruit alone is distinguished by a color of blood, which develops itself gradually and like flakes. When the fruit begins to ripen it is like other oranges; little by little, spots of blood-color appear in its pulp; as it advances to maturity, these enlarge, becoming deeper, and finally embrace all the pulp and spread to the skin, which is, however, but rarely covered by the peculiar color; yet this sometimes occurs if oranges are left upon the trees after the month of May.

This orange is multiplied only by grafts, having few seeds, and those of little value. This is a proof that it is a monster; if it were the type of a species it would yield more seed and reproduce itself by seed. Its branches are without thorns, its fruit is sweet, but less so than the China orange, and it has thicker skin.

It is cultivated largely in Malta and Provence. In Liguria it is found chiefly among amateurs and seedsmen.—*Gallesio.*

So far as the Florida Fruit Growers' Association has determined, through their committee, the nomenclature of our own varieties it is given below, and such should be authority among the growers in Florida.

Citron—Common.—Fruit very large ; color that of ordinary lemon ; rind and pulp white, and almost tasteless ; tree vigorous.

Orange Citron.—Fruit somewhat cone-shaped, more pointed than common variety ; color that of an ordinary orange ; rind cream-colored ; pulp yellowish ; rind sweet and highly aromatic ; fruit possesses less bitterness than the common variety ; tree a small, stiff, erect grower. For home use or commercial purposes this variety is in general cultivation.

Tangierine Orange; synonyms, *Mandarin, Kid Glove, Tomato Orange.*—Size medium ; much flattened ; color dark orange ; broad, irregular cavity, with stem obliquely inserted and surrounded by a knobbed eminence ; eye set in a large depression one inch wide and five sixteenths deep ; longitudinal diameter two and a half inches, transverse diameter three inches ; skin irregularly ribbed or lobed ; color of flesh very dark orange ; pulp adhering to skin by a few filaments ; sections of pulp easily separated ; pulp coarse ; juice sweet and highly aromatic ; aroma marked ; quality first. Tree of original variety introduced by Major Atway, from Bayou Sara, La., and now growing in the grove of Dr. Moragne, at Palatka.

Dancy's Tangierine.—Size small ; much flattened ; color deeper and more brilliant than parent variety ; longitudinal diameter one and three quarter inches, transverse diameter two and one quarter inches ; the eye set in a deep cavity seven eighths in diameter ;

stalk straight and inserted in a ribbed depression; thickness of the skin three sixteenths; general properties of pulp same as parent, only superior; fruit nearly seedless. In flavor and external appearance this variety is superior to the original. Seminal variety of the Tangierine raised by Colonel F. L. Dancy, Buena Vista, St. Johns county, Fla.

Citrus Japonica; synonym, *Dwarf Orange.*—Dwarf-growing variety; size of fruit small; slightly obovate; color deep orange; skin thin; eye set in a flattened depression; fruit regularly ribbed or lobed; longitudinal diameter two inches, transverse diameter one inch and seven eighths; color of flesh dark; grain fine and tender; juice very acid. Useless, except as an ornamental fruit.

Navel Orange; synonyms, *Umbilical, Bahia, Pernambuco, Seedless Orange, Embiguo.*—Size large to very large; eye presenting an umbilical appearance (from which it obtains its name); stem inserted in a shallow-ribbed cavity with deep lines; skin three sixteenths thick; longitudinal diameter three and five eighths, transverse three and three quarters; flesh very fine, melting, and tender; juice sweet, sprightly, vinous, and aromatic; quality first. Origin, Bahia, Brazil.

Citrus Myrtifolia.—Myrtle-leaved orange; fruit small and slightly flattened; eye set in flattened depression; leaves like those of the myrtle; flavor resembling that of a bitter-sweet. Fruit useless for table.

Sweet Seville (*Hicks'*).—Size small; slightly flattened; color comparatively deep; eye small, without depression; skin very smooth; thickness of skin two sixteenths; longitudinal diameter two inches, transverse two and three eighths; color darker than Navel orange; foliage differs from other varieties examined; leaves markedly obovate; average length about three and one quarter inches; width about two and five eighths; grain very fine, juicy, and melting; juice very sweet and sprightly; quality best; a superior fruit in every respect except size. Supposed to be a seedling raised at Arcadia, St. John's county, Florida.

Arcadia.—Size large; form somewhat flattened; color deep; eye set in slight depression; stalk inserted in a slight roughened cavity; skin smooth with marked pits; thickness of skin three sixteenths; longitudinal diameter two and three quarter inches; transverse diameter three and a quarter inches; color of flesh deep; grain coarse; pulp melting; juice slightly sub-acid; quality good. Supposed seedling raised at Arcadia, and introduced by the Rev. William Watkin Hicks.

Bergamot.—Form flattened, with projecting nipple; color deep lemon; eye absent, and its place occupied by a nipple-like projection; stem inserted in a slight depression; skin two sixteenths; longitudinal diameter through nipple three inches, transverse three inches; color of pulp nearly white; juice sweet and watery without any decided flavor; rind possesses a pear-like fragrance, from which perfumers obtain their bergamot essences. Only worthy of cultivation as a curiosity.

Nonpareil.—Size about medium; somewhat flattened; color ordinary; eye broad and set in a slightly depressed cavity; stem inserted in a level, scarred surface; skin three sixteenths thick; longitudinal diameter two and three quarters of an inch ; transverse diameter three and a quarter ; color of flesh ordinary ; grain fine ; pulp melting and tender ; juice sub-acid and vinous ; quality good. Seedling raised by Mrs. Mary Richard, Arlington River, Duval County, Florida.

Magnum Bonum.—Size large to very large ; flattened ; color light-clear orange ; eye set in a slight cavity ; stem inserted in a narrow depression ; skin smooth and glossy ; thickness of skin two sixteenths ; longitudinal three inches, and the transverse three and five eighths ; color of flesh light ; grain very fine, tender, and melting ; fruit very heavy and juicy ; juice sweet, rich, and vinous ; quality best. Probably a seedling raised at Homosassa, Fla., the former residence of the Hon. Mr. Yulee.

Old Vini.—Size about medium ; slightly flattened ; color dark orange ; eye broad, and set in a slight cavity ; stem inserted in a narrow wrinkled depression ; surface of skin rough ; thickness of skin three sixteenths ; longitudinal diameter two and three quarter inches ; transverse diameter three and one eighth ; grain coarse ; pulp melting ; juice sub-acid and remarkable for a sprightly vinous property ; quality good. Seedling raised by Col. Dancy, Buena Vista, St. John's County, Florida.

Buena Vista ; synonym, *Sweet Seville.*—Size medium ; slightly flattened ; color dark crimson ; eye set in a slightly depressed cavity ; stem inserted in a slight depression ; skin smooth, with deep pits ; thickness of skin nearly four sixteenths ; longitudinal diameter two and three quarter inches, transverse three inches ; color of flesh very dark ; pulp coarse, but melting; juice sub-acid; sprightly with vinous flavor; quality good. Seedling raised by Colonel Dancy.

No. 3 (Beach's).—Size above medium; form oblong; color light; eye set in flattened surface; stem inserted in a slight, wrinkled cavity; thickness of skin three sixteenths; longitudinal diameter three and three eighths, transverse three and a quarter inches; pulp coarse, not melting; juice sub-acid; quality fair.

Osceola.—Size large; slightly flattened; color bright; skin smooth and glossy; eye very small, and set in a slight cavity; stem inserted in small, shallow, wrinkled depression; skin three sixteenths thick; longitudinal diameter three inches; transverse three and a quarter; grain coarse; pulp rather melting; juice sweet; quality good. Seedling raised by L. H. Van Pelt, Mandarin, Florida.

Dixon Orange.—Size large; somewhat flattened; color light; eye small, inserted in a slightly depressed cavity; stem inserted in deep, narrow depression; thickness of skin four sixteenths of an inch; longitudinal diameter three inches; transverse three and a half; grain coarse; pulp not melting; juice sub-acid, without any decided flavor; quality second. Seedling raised on Indian River.

Sweet Seville (Tolman's).—Size below medium, but larger than Hicks' variety; form flattened; color light orange; eye large, without any cavity, and surrounded by a dark circle; stem inserted without cavity; skin smooth and two sixteenths thick; longitudinal diameter two and a quarter inches, transverse two and five eighths; pulp fine, melting, juicy, sweet; inferior quality to Hicks' variety. Origin, Mandarin, Florida.

Sweet Lemon. —Size very small; form much flattened; color rusty, grayish yellow; instead of eye a marked nipple set in a deep cavity; stem inserted in a slight depression; thickness of skin two sixteenths; longitudinal diameter two inches, transverse two and one eighth; color of flesh dark lemon; grain of pulp coarse; juice sweet and insipid, with slight lemon flavor. Curious, but unworthy of cultivation.

The following appeared in the Florida *Agriculturist*, from the pen of A. H. Manville, one of our most intelligent nurserymen:

SELECTION OF VARIETIES.

In planting for profit it would be almost impossible for a person unacquainted with the many varieties of the citrus to make an intelligent selection without a more comprehensive guide than a brief description of the different varieties.

Of the varieties of the Sweet Orange known in Florida, the Bell, Du Roi, Egg, Blood, and Navel are distinctly marked and readily distinguishable by their appearance. The Bell — which must not be confounded with the insipid, thick-skinned, early, oblong variety—and the Du Roi are in every respect superior fruit; their fine quality will always command for them a high price, while their distinctive characteristics will prevent deception or confusion regarding their variety. The Navel ranks among the first for size and quality; and, like the above, its peculiar mark will distinguish it in market. Unlike the above, it is not a prolific bearer, on which account many fear to plant; it is however by no means as shy a bearer as has been represented. The Blood has not been fruited long enough in the State to determine its market value. The Egg is valuable as an early fruit for home use; its small size and want of flavor render it unfit for market. The Sweet Seville and St. Michaels, though not distinctly marked, are to some extent distinguishable by the appearance of the fruit; the former is one of the most delicious for home use, though too small for profitable shipment; the latter is prolific and a good market fruit. Acis, Arcadia, Beach's No. 3, Creole, Dummit, Dixon, Excelsior, HAMOSASSA, Higgins, MAGNUM BONUM, NONPAREIL, Osceola, OLD VINI, PEERLESS, Ahiti, and perhaps others having a local name and celebrity, are native varieties recently brought to public notice; those in SMALL CAPS are best known and most highly esteemed. They are all very similar, the difference, if any, being too slight to distinguish them in market, and of little importance to growers generally. The differences of description have arisen from soil, location, and treatment rather than from any intrinsic difference in the fruit. This multiplication of varieties differing little in character would seem at first to be useless, confusing the grower and burdening the nurserymen; in fact, they served good purposes, placing a superior variety within reach of every section, and being a safeguard against the numberless inferior sorts. While, therefore, it is immaterial in planting which of these be selected, it is highly important that a well-known accredited variety be chosen. Tardiff does not differ in appearance or quality from the above, but retains its perfection until very late in the season ; if this habit remains permanent it will be one of the most desirable. Botelha, Dulcissima, Jaffa, and other recently imported varieties have not been fruited long enough in the State to determine their qualities.

Of all the citrus tribe the Mandarin or Tangerine orange is the most delicate and aromatic, though scarcely as luscious as the Sweet Orange of Florida. On account of its beautiful shape, color, and the ease with which the rind and segments separate, it is highly esteemed as a dessert fruit. Comparatively few are shipped, and these bring an enormously high price. The effect of increased production consequent upon the large number being planted remains to be seen. The trees are hardy and prolific. There are two distinct classes—the first dwarfed, willow-leaved, and yellow-fruited. Of this class there are many inferior seedling varieties which have occasioned a prejudice against it in some localities ; the trees can be planted much closer than the Sweet Orange. The second, full-sized, large-leaved, crimson-fruited, much prized on account of its color. The China and St. Michaels of the former class and the Bijou of the latter are superior varieties.

Until recently Florida lemons have been regarded as too large, thick-skinned, and bitter-rinded for profitable shipment. The last few years have demonstrated this to be erroneous. Heretofore comparatively unknown in market, a poor opinion was formed from the inferior quality and improper preparation of the specimens fowarded. The fruit is now in demand, sought for by local buyers and consignees in Northern markets, and commands a price equal to the best Florida oranges and much greater than imported lemons. As a result of this favorable condition of market, many are planting extensively. The lemon is more prolific and an earlier bearer than the orange, and its cultivation equally or more remunerative; the tree will not stand as great a degree of cold as the latter, but is successfully grown as far north as Putnam County. While much of the fruit produced in the State is superior in quality, there are numberless coarse, inferior sorts; to avoid these, as with the orange, only well-known leading varieties should be planted. The Sicily, or imported lemon of commerce, French's Seedling, not the so-called French lemon, and Lamb have fruited for some years, and are far superior in every respect, the two latter being equal to the imported fruit. The characteristics of the fruit of these three varieties are essentially the same. French's Seedling is less thorny than the others. Bijou, Eureka, Genoa, Imperial, and some others recently introduced promise well. Ever-bearing is valuable for home use rather than market. Young trees of this species, even of the best varieties, are apt to produce large, coarse fruit; it becomes smaller and finer as the tree grows older.

Extract from Horticultural Congress Papers, by Thomas Rivers, England.

Botelha and *Dulcissima*, both thin rinds and very rich. *Egg*, very large, rind thick, remarkably juicy, but not rich; a great bearer. *Exquisite*, a thin-rinded, rich, and juicy fruit. *Maltese Blood*, large, oval, with dark red pulp, exceedingly rich, good and distinct; fruit from the same tree vary in color from deep red to the usual pale yellow color, with faint streaks of red. *St. Michaels*, thin rind, very juicy, and bears abundantly. *Silver Orange*, color of rind pale yellow, flesh pale, rind very thin, flavor piquant and delicious. *Sustain*, large, and remarkable for its sweet juices. *White Orange*, large, rind pale yellow, flesh very pale, flavor rich and good.

The following is from the report of the Southern California Horticultural Society:

FINE ORANGES.

T. A. Garey, from San Francisco, presented several specimens of Garey's Mediterranean Sweet Orange, to show in what a good state of preservation this fruit will keep to so late a period as the middle of August. The specimens were cut and tested by those present. They were of a fine texture, solid, juicy, of a good flavor, and looked as though they would remain on the trees unimpaired in quality for a month longer. Mr. Garey claims for this fruit the following good qualities:

This orange commences to fruit the second year from the bud.

It bears heavy and regular crops.

The fruit commences to ripen in December, and remains sound and firm on the tree until the following August.

It is of large size, symmetrical shape, and extraordinary fine color.

A large proportion are entirely seedless.

The flavor is excellent, the grain very fine, and the fruit is almost entirely free from the tough and stringy membranous substances usually found in oranges.

Its keeping qualities are superior to any variety tested in this country, rendering it a superior market fruit.

The tree is a rapid grower, symmetrical in shape, and forming invariably a round and beautiful head.

An entire absence of thorns, avoiding by this peculiarity the large percentage of loss usually sustained in the puncturing of the fruit by the thorns or spines found on the common variety of orange trees.

In concluding this subject of varieties, I would urge upon the orange growers of this State the advisability of selecting and cultivating varieties with reference to their time of maturing. The orange naturally has the advantage of most fruits in point of extending the time of ripening. It is a crop that can be harvested as the market demands—beginning ordinarily with November and ending with March. And this period might be extended so as to embrace a still longer time, by gathering in March and carefully housing, thus preventing deterioration of fruit by longer hanging on the tree, and giving relief to the latter.

This course has been advised by one who has studied the methods of handling the orange in European groves.

A dry packing-house, with numerous shelves and frequent fumigation, will probably play an important part in the future as a preventive of a temporary market-glut, or the effects of a septennial freeze. But this matter can be helped by an intelligent selection of kinds for stocking a grove. Nor have we even then seen the final result: if early varieties have been propagated in this initiatory stage of the study of the orange industry, others will be introduced that are earlier; if a freak of nature has given us an orange that ripens in March, the observant orchardist will not be long in improving on this.

A late-maturing orange has already been mentioned in these pages, but there is an early variety that nurserymen pass over in their catalogues, yet which should not be despised. Like the lemon grown in this State, its treatment has not been such as to bring out its merits. Under no circumstances is it as good an orange as the ordinary Florida fruit, when the latter is matured. But the "Thornless Bell" is edible in September, and is best when gathered then, before it yellows on the tree. When permitted to turn on the tree it loses that sufficiency of acidity which it possesses earlier, and which prevents its being insipid—the common objection to it. Instead of a thick rind, it then cures with a skin as thin as that of the imported Sicily orange, and with which it will probably compare favorably as to general quality. Let it be understood that all that is claimed for this "September" orange, as it might be designated, are its early ripening qualities and its wonderfully prolific nature.

CHAPTER XVIII.

THE LEMON AND LIME.

COMPARATIVELY little attention has been given in Florida to the cultivation of the lemon and lime; and yet these are among the most valuable of the citrus family, whether we consider their monetary value or their healthfulness. This neglect has arisen from several causes.

The lemon is a more vigorous grower than the orange, and when planted on strong or fresh land the fruit grows to a much larger size and with a thicker skin than in Europe. The rind, also, when the fruit is permitted to yellow upon the tree, is bitter, which destroys the commercial value of the lemon. Other ill results are noticed when the fruit is permitted to ripen on the tree. Such fruit is comparatively light, the juice sparse, and charged with a small per cent of citric acid. All this is the result of a want of knowledge of proper treatment of the fruit. My lemons have brought in New York and Philadelphia more money per box than my oranges, and have in these markets ranked as first quality. I would mention also that as a general rule the lemon tree is more productive than the orange. This fruit which ranked so high was gathered from seedlings planted from seed of the Sicily and Messina fruit of commerce. If the fruit on these trees is allowed to ripen on the tree they average three fourths of a pound in weight, but of inferior quality, juice little, and rind thick.

My method of prèparing for market is to gather the fruit when about one third larger than we find the Sicily lemon when it reaches our American market. In curing, the fruit will shrink this extra third. The fruit is gathered in latticed boxes holding about fifty lemons each and only two layers deep. The fruit should be cut with short stems, and so handled as not to be bruised. The boxes are at once put into a close room one on top of another, but forming a hollow square. If the room is large, cover the pile of boxes with a cloth that will confine the sulphurous gas with which the fruit is to be treated. Place in the centre of the square, and sufficiently remote from the boxes not to heat the fruit, an oven of live coals. Throw on the burning coals an ounce of flowers of sulphur, and fasten down the cloths. If the room is small and tight the cloth is not necessary. Allow the fruit to remain in a dark room for a week, then expose to sunlight—the direct rays of the sun a part of the day is best—until the skin is yellow. The fruit is then ready for market or to be stored for future use, for when thus treated it can be kept for an indefinite time. This sulphurous gas is of great benefit in the curing of both lemon and orange : First, it aids in properly curing the fruit by toughening the skin and drying up the watery particles; second, it is fatal to all parasites of the orange, whether vegetable or animal. I am satisfied that a very large per cent of the speedy decay of the orange so fatal to shippers is occasioned by the germs of fungi left over from the former year in packing-houses, and old boxes in which rotten fruit was conveyed. These germs lie dormant, waiting for a moist atmosphere favorable to their development; they then develop and multiply with wondrous rapidity, showing their work in the form of mould on any moist surface, but especially on fruit. Some years ago I put into a basket that had held some decayed lemons, on the sides of which basket at the time of gathering I noticed a little mould, some very fine Tangerine oranges. In two days' time half the fruit was entirely worthless. The fruit that was left on the tree, or that had been otherwise handled, was entirely sound. This gave me a hint. It was a very wet season; most of our shippers were losing heavily. Commission merchants were constantly reporting "Fruit arrived in bad order," "Did not pay expenses." I knew that sulphurous fumes were fatal to fungoids. I commenced to gather and ship in the midst of the damp season. I fumigated every box of fruit, and though mould had appeared on the fruit as it hung on the trees, I heard no report of decayed fruit, but on the contrary had the report of "Arrived in good condition," and "Good price."

I have not had much experience in handling the lime, but I am convinced that this fruit, most valuable because of its healthfulness and its richness in citric acid, can be cured as easily as the lemon, and preserved quite as long if subjected to the treatment recommended for the lemon. This fruit needs only to be known in our Northern market to be valued even more highly than the lemon. When once brought into notice it will prove truly profitable to the grower. The yield is speedy and abundant.

The Florida lemon, marketed during the latter part of August and all of September and October, meets with little competition from foreign fruit.

CHAPTER XIX.

THE INSECTS DAMAGING TO THE ORANGE TREE—THE NATURAL ENEMIES OF SUCH INSECTS, AND THE REMEDIES TO BE APPLIED.

BUT few insects injurious to the orange tree have appeared, but their ravages have now and then done considerable mischief, and awakened still greater apprehension. The insect which at one time was considered the most injurious was the long scale insect, resembling one side of a distorted muscle-shell, and was called by Packard Aspidiotus Gloverii. When it first made its appearance in Florida it threatened universal destruction of the orange groves. It first made its appearance at Mandarin, Florida, about forty years ago, to which place it was brought on some China orange plants freshly imported from China. The insect is very diminutive, and under a glass of strong power has the appearance of a white louse. It is very quick in its motions (its movements resembling those of the chicken-mite), and conceals itself, during the presence of an enemy, under the scale erected for the shelter, first of the egg and then of the young insect. The eggs are purple and laid in two parallel rows. The insect when hatched at once begins to suck the sap—like the aphis—from the bark and leaf of the tree wherever the scale happens to be fastened. It finally develops into a diminutive fly undiscoverable with the natural eye, except when late in the afternoon they can be seen between the observer and the declining sun when the tree infested is suddenly jarred. The effect produced by their sucking is first to deplete and finally to exhaust and kill the branch and leaf to which they cling. Several remedies have been found effectual. The most effective yet known to the writer is a decoction of tobacco with sufficient carbolic soap to make a strong suds. Apply with a garden syringe or pump, through a perforated nozzle. Kerosene, in the proportion of one part of kerosene to eleven of water, applied in the same manner, is effective. But there is danger if too much be used. A moderate amount is a good fertilizer and stimulant to the tree. As there is no chemical affinity between the kerosene and water, the mixture has to be kept vigorously stirred during the time of applying it. Either of these applications has to be repeated two or three times, at intervals of ten or twelve days.

Another insect similar to the one just considered, but with scale of lighter appearance and of rounder form, is also damaging to the trees. This insect seldom attacks either the leaves or the tender wood, but confines itself mainly to the bark of the wood from one to four years old. They are easily and effectively removed by washing the trunks with wood-ashes and water in the proportion of one quart of ashes to three gallons of water. If found generally on the tree in positions not easily reached by the hand, syringe as before with "white lye"—lye prepared by boiling wood-ashes.

A most formidable enemy to both these insects named has appeared within the last two years in the grove of the writer. It is a lady-bug with a single red spot on each wing case. In both the pupa and perfect state it is ever busy devouring these insects. Of course they are allowed full freedom of the grove, and are increasing very rapidly.

Another enemy, noticed for the first time and during the present year in the grove of the writer, of the long scale insect, has appeared in the form of a small hang or basket worm, "named by Mr. Packard (as the writer has been informed through the entomological department of the Agricultural Department), Platœcitus Gloverii," but later named Psyche Confederata. The female remains in her case and devours insects inclosed under her web. The male is a small dark-colored moth. These insects are not a very formidable enemy to the scale, as the female confines herself closely in her operations under her web. But some small trees have been entirely rid of insects by their help. But if "these insects," as the entomologist of the Agricultural Department writes, "in their habits resemble the basket or drop worm of the North," they might prove an enemy to the orange tree as well as to the scale insect, and if so should not be encouraged.

Another insect resembles, when young, fine corn-meal dusted over the tree, but when the case in which the insects are inclosed is full grown it resembles the small barnacles clinging to a wharf built in salt water. When these cases are turned over and examined with a glass they disclose under each a multitude of small insects resembling lice. They do not exhaust trees so rapidly as the scale insect, but their presence is damaging. The leaves of the trees infested change after a while to a dark sooty appearance, and the tree does not grow so rapidly.

An enemy to this insect also has appeared. I am informed by the entomologist of the Agricultural Department, to whom I sent specimens of this and the other insects mentioned, that the "insect is the Evagoras Rubidus, which destroys the plant-lice on the cotton and orange, at least I have found it in the act of sucking out the juice of a plant-louse." As I finished the above sentence I laid my pen down to go out and capture some of these insects, that I might give a more accurate description, and found a full-grown insect which had just pierced with his proboscis a full-grown house-fly. He continued his feast for a few moments as I watched, and when frightened retreated, carrying his prey with him. This insect when young resembles a red spider. As it increases in size it changes to a salmon color with white spots. When half grown, or about one half inch in length, two small black wings are visible. When full grown, or three fourths of an inch in length, two pairs of wings show themselves, the smaller or under pair black, the upper pair black, with salmon-colored marking on the forward halves of the wings. When fully grown the insect is ready for flight and is very active. When young it is very busy feeding upon *small* insects ; when grown it seeks for larger prey. Since writing the above I find a description of the above insect in Agricultural Report of 1875, page 131.

The wood-louse, or white ant, has occasioned serious trouble and sometimes death to many fine young trees where the preventive was not used— ashes or slaked lime around the base of the trunk. When a tree begins suddenly to show yellow leaves examine a few inches below the surface at the base of the trunk for wood-lice, especially if a stake has been driven near the tree for its support, or if litter from the forest or mulching of leaves has been used. If wood-lice are discovered, clear them away carefully, and pour boiling water into the cavity around the tree until all the cavities in which the lice could have concealed themselves have been reached. If the tree has been but partially girdled it will recover, if the soil be placed above the wounded part. But if the tree has been completely girdled, get well rotted muck and pile it for three or four inches above the wound, and cover over with sand. Finish with a top-dressing of fresh wood-ashes or slaked lime. If the tree is not too far spent it will send out young roots above the wound and finally recover.

Another insect to be noticed resembles the squash-bug, and is called by the entomologist of the Department of Agriculture Euthoctha Galeator. This insect is very bold in its attack. I have watched them frequently in their operations as they were lying in the hot sun basking, while their proboscs were inserted in the tender shoots. I have held my magnifying-glass within a half or three quarters of an inch from them, and had the finest opportunity of observing the operations of this bold enemy of the orange. I have seen the tenderer shoots wilt when the insect was sucking them, from the extremity to the point at which this insect had inserted its proboscis. As this insect is large, the injury inflicted by it is speedy. But when the shoot is older and more vigorous the effect is very similar to that produced by die-back. These insects are more apt to attack trees starting young shoots at periods of the year when the grove is not generally making new wood. As they cannot pierce the old wood they seek for the tenderest. This accounts for the impression that *stimulating* or forcing a tree produces the die-back.

The Euthoctha Galeator is fond of concealing itself under litter of any kind during the night or cold weather. Mulching around a tree is an attractive covert from which they start forth, when the sun begins to shine warmly, to the nearest tender branch. This has caused others to conclude that *mulching* was the cause of die-back.

There is another form of this disease, arising from an entirely different cause, to be noticed in the next chapter. As no natural enemies of these insects are known, watchfulness on the part of the orange grower is alone to be relied upon for their destruction. They should be caught by hand or in a net and killed. The insect last described is very apt to conceal itself under litter during the winter. Pieces of bark, boards, logs, stumps, litter of every kind offer them shelter. In early spring when the weather is cold everything of the kind in the vicinity of the orange grove infested should be burned. The insect is very fond of sucking the cow-pea, and lays its eggs near its field of operation, often on the under side of the leaf of the plant on which it feeds. If the orange grower will grow cow-peas in his grove and bury them in trenches or holes dug at the extremity of the orange roots, a few days after these insects have commenced to feed upon the peas, he can destroy them at a most important time. Both these plans were adopted by the writer during the present year, and his grove is now quite clear of this pest.

When trees have been damaged seriously by these insects the knife and saw must be freely used.

Cut away all diseased wood. Let the cutting be so heavy that the tree will start strong shoots. Watch these young shoots carefully, when the sun is warm, for the bug resembling the squash-bug. Kill all that make their appearance. If the extremities of the shoots have been stung, pinch them back. They cannot be saved if the wood is very tender. If blisters appear in the harder wood, puncture them with a knife. It will relieve the wood, which will readily heal, and the branch will soon recover its vigor.

The writer has allowed some trees to go almost to the last extremity, and brought them out by following the above plan.

The most effective insecticide known to the author is kerosene and soap—whale-oil soap being preferable—but if this is not convenient, common washing-soap is effective—combined in the proportions of six pounds of soap to one gallon of kerosene. Bring the soap to a boil, pour in the kerosene and stir thoroughly until the two are fully combined.

This preparation can be diluted with water to suit the character of the insects to be exterminated.

As an ordinary wash, forty gallons of water added to the above preparation will leave the solution sufficiently strong.

For the red scale insect not more than twenty gallons of water should be added.

Some prefer an emulsion of kerosene and milk diluted with water.

CHAPTER XX.

DISEASES TO WHICH THE ORANGE TREE AND FRUIT ARE LIABLE, AND THEIR REMEDIES.

FEW fruit trees are less liable to disease than the orange, but the fruit and trees are so valuable that no enemy should be allowed to attack them unopposed. Perhaps the most formidable disease which has yet made its appearance is the "die-back." One cause producing this disease has already been noticed in a preceding chapter. The name "die-back" is a general term, used for want of a better and more specific name or names, for at least two diseases arising from three and perhaps four different causes. But as it is descriptive of the symptoms of one or more diseases arising from several different causes, its meaning is readily comprehended. The symptom is the dying back of the new wood to the old. It is sometimes confined to a few branches of the tree. When this is the case the inference is that it is caused solely from the sting of an insect. If, however, the symptom is general to the young branches, and they come forth feeble and yellow with no marks of stings, the cause *may* originate near the roots.

Deep planting will produce such symptoms.

Trees do not depend solely upon their leaves for the supply of carbonic acid. The roots gather a very considerable part of this gas, so essential to plant life, not in a pure state, as is done by the leaf, but in chemical combination with other elements. This is the case especially with trees which have very yellow roots. Such trees send their roots either into a very porous soil easily penetrated by the air, or else send them near the surface, where they find a greater abundance of air, which decomposes manure and is essential to the formation of carbonic acid. Such is the case with the orange tree and roots. If the tree is planted too deep or the crust on the top of the soil has become very compact, these roots, dependent upon air for health and ability to perform their functions, are virtually smothered. They make an effort to grow, but as often as they form rootlets and root-hairs, these die and convey no nutriment for the formation of the *woody* structure of young shoots, so the new and tender cells, which are but the frame-work of the plant, perish for want of support. And hence the light cellular structure, in the form of young shoots, dies back as certainly as if it had been cut from the older wood. I have occasionally dug up trees so afflicted and found them wanting in new roots. The remedy is to reset, or else take away the top soil till the lateral roots are brought near the surface, and to keep the soil well cultivated. Cut away all diseased wood and roots. When the extremities of roots of trees come in contact with poisonous earth or fermenting manures, a similar symptom is produced, as in planting upon hard-pan or over a stratum of salt earth.

Where moss appears on the trunks of trees, it is easily removed by any alkali wash. Soap-suds, or what is better, wood-ashes, will both fertilize and cleanse.

The cracking of the fruit is occasioned by any suspension of the growth of the fruit, and a consequent hardening of the rind, followed by a sudden flow of sap from any stimulating cause, as highly fertilizing a bearing grove, especially during summer, or a wet spell following a dry. This cracking is more apt to follow the rains, if trees have been highly manured even in winter. This can be prevented by keeping the ground well stirred during dry weather. The soil thus stirred absorbs moisture and keeps the fruit growing.

Two other diseases have of late years shown themselves in Florida, and occasioned great fear and trouble among orange growers. One is known as the "foot-rot." The symptoms are the decay and sloughing of the bark around the crown and tap-roots of the tree. I have had no experience in my own grove with this disease, but have watched its effects in many portions of the State. It has occasioned much trouble and loss in Louisiana, from whose orange growers I have had many letters of inquiry, some of whom have confounded the disease with another, presently to be mentioned. I am convinced that this trouble is occasioned by one general cause—the fermenting of sap in the vicinity of the "rot." The sap of the orange abounds in oil and starch, which, in combination with watery particles, favor easy and rapid fermentation, especially when the circulation is slow. So far as I have discovered, this fermentation is induced mainly from two causes—first, fermenting manures around the base of the trunk. Of course, this should not be allowed. Second, stagnant water around the roots. If water is allowed to flow or drain slowly from the ground it is not likely to ferment. I have known it to flow for weeks above the surface of the ground with no seeming damage to the trees, but if allowed to stand on the surface, or a little below the surface, under the influence of a powerful sun fermentation speedily sets in, and a few weeks or months thereafter the roots of the tree resting therein begin to show signs of decay. The first symptom is a darkening of the sap, next loosening of the bark of the roots, and last rot of bark. The prevention is, to underdrain, and keep the crown-roots well exposed to air and sunlight. If underdraining is impracticable, carry off the surface water and keep the ground well mulched, that a lower temperature may check the tendency to fermentation. In localities where this disease is troublesome, sour stock, as it is better adapted to wet and acid soils, do better than the sweet stock.

The other disease to which reference has been made is "bleeding," an exudation of sap, hardening into gum, from the trunk of the tree. As this trouble is more frequent after a severe winter, I am persuaded it is occasioned by a rupture of the sap-vessels, inducing, as in "foot-rot," fermentation beneath the bark, under which the diseased sap collects, first forming a blister and then breaking through the bark, corroding and hardening into gum. The remedy is to cut away the diseased bark as far as there is any discoloration of sap, and whitewash the wound, or apply fresh cow-dung. Thus treated, if the cutting has been to the sound bark, the wound soon heals. It is not infrequently the case that the bug, the same or similar to the one that stings the deadened pine tree, attracted by the fermenting sap, deposits its egg beneath the bark. This egg develops into a borer which feeds upon the fermenting wood, and may sometimes extend his operations into the sound wood. But the presence of this borer is the result and not the cause of the disease. When this invader appears he must be hunted and taken out with the knife. Dead limbs or dead wood on a tree will invite a similar borer, which feeds on the dry wood of either the orange or oak, but I have not known of this insect doing any damage to the growing wood.

CHAPTER XXI.

RUST ON THE ORANGE.

RUST has been the cause of considerable annoyance to the growers of the orange in Florida. The writer has for years been engaged in experiments for the purpose of ascertaining, first, the cause of, and then the remedy for, the rust. Some years ago he reached the conclusion that the rust was nothing more than the oxidized oil from the skin spread over the surface. This discovery was first made through the microscope, and afterward confirmed by chemical tests. The cause of exudation of oil was first attributed to some peculiar condition of the soil. Different remedies were applied with the hope of getting rid of such matter as would produce an excess of hydrocarbonates. Among other things, caustic lime was applied broadcast through the orangery. The rust disappeared for two or three years, and again returned. Eighteen months ago the writer's attention was called, by Mr. W. C. Hargrove, of Palatka, to a microscopic insect first noticed by Mr. J. K. Gates, and believed by them to be the cause of the rust.

This led me to investigate in another direction. Knowing Mr. William H. Ashmead, of Jacksonville,

Fla., to be investigating orange insects, I sought his co-operation. He found the insect new to entomologists, but belonging to the order Acarina, and family Phytoptidæ. Mr. Ashmead gave to the insect the name Phytoptus oleivorous, or oil-eating. He has given a very interesting chapter on the subject in his pamphlet on "Orange Insects." The writer, during the two summers last past, has tried a number of experiments, hoping to find a destroyer of the insect and a preventive of rust. He found a strong decoction of tobacco with whale-oil soap, one pound to ten gallons of the decoction, the most effective. This decoction was applied by means of a pump, forcing the liquid through a rose nozzle and drenching the foliage and fruit. The application should be made monthly during May, June, and July, as there are monthly generations of the insect. The present year I found them attached to the fruit as late as October. When there is no fruit on the trees the insects attach themselves to the leaves. Lime, sown broadcast when foliage is damp, is beneficial.

The insect is microscopic, and only discoverable with the unaided eye when they are in great abundance upon the fruit or leaves. Then the fruit and leaves have the appearance of having been slightly dusted with the finest flour. I copy description from Mr. Ashmead's work: "Whitish flesh-color, elongated; gradually increasing in size near the head it becomes twice as thick as posteriorly; abdomen finely and transversely striate, apparently consisting of numerous very thin segments; at the extremity is a biped appendage that evidently assists it in clinging to the orange; just above it protrude two caudal filaments; head almost hidden in thorax; four legs rather short with one claw, a long hair springing from the knee."

When the insect attacks the orange before the fruit is grown it is dwarfed in size and blackened; when attacked later, the color is changed to a dark bronze; if still later, to a light bronze. The fruit is not otherwise damaged by the "rust." Some claim a benefit from the rust, since "rusted" fruit keeps better and is shipped with less damage. Such fruit is also sweeter, as the watery particles are allowed to escape through the punctured skin and the saccharine matter thus concentrated. As the oil exudes from the punctures made by the insect and spreads over the surface, it hardens into a varnish which protects the fruit against atmospheric influences.

The most available time to attack the rust insect is during the winter, before the trees have put on their new crop of fruit. At that time the insect has fastened itself to the under side of the leaf. It does not transfer itself to the fruit until the oil-cells are well formed. By lodging on the under side of the leaf it is more difficult to attack. But if caustic and well-slaked lime is applied when the leaves are well dampened with dew (dew is better than the rain, as the rain does not wet the under side of the leaf) the fine particles of lime adhere to the leaves and destroy the insect. The application should be made from beneath the tree, the operator standing near the trunk and throwing the lime in handfuls up among the branches. The same rule should be observed when the tree is washed with a decoction of tobacco and whale-oil soap. It should be first syringed from beneath; afterward it may be showered from the side, and thus by drenching every part of the tree insure a more effectual application and remedy.

Another reason why the application of remedies should be made in winter is, the insect does not seem to be multiplying during the colder weather. It certainly is much more active during the warmer months. It should be attacked when at a disadvantage. Every tree in the grove should be treated, and if possible every leaf of every tree in the grove. What would be better still, communities ought to combine and operate at the same time, that the enemy may be exterminated. When once they have obtained a lodgment in a grove they multiply very rapidly during a hot dry spell. An opinion prevails that wet weather increases the rust. This is true to a limited extent. The oil does not exude from the punctures made by the insect till it has removed itself from the puncture or died. As long as it continues to suck the oil the orange does not rust. Should the orange be stimulated to active circulation of sap, the pressure from within induces a more active flow of oil. Hence the rain makes the show of rust the more speedy by first stimulating to an increased flow of oil and then hastening its oxidizing. The rust does not appear simultaneously with the insect, but follows its operations. Hot weather is favorable to the development of the insect, but wet weather increases the show of rust.

Sulphate of lime I have found to be a specific for the rust-insect. Two applications should be made during the year, one in the spring before the blooming of the trees, the other during the month of June. The sulphate of lime or land plaster should be applied while the tree is wet, at the rate of from one to two quarts to the tree. The whole of the trunk, branches, and foliage should be well dusted.

CHAPTER XXII.

GATHERING, PACKING, AND SHIPPING THE ORANGE.

IN Europe these branches of the business belong to the merchant, and are studied as an art. The merchant buys the fruit on the trees either in bulk or by the thousand, counting 1040 as an M. But in this country, and especially thus early in the history of orange growing, it is well for the grower to understand this part of his business so well that he can gather, pack, and ship his own fruit without being left to the mercy of speculators, many of whom are concerned only so far as they may get the greater part of the profits. Ignorance of these things has already occasioned large annual loss both to the producer and buyer. The oranges from many groves have generally been *pulled* off, the rinds of many torn in gathering them from the tree, and these oranges piled into a boat or cart and offered in bulk upon the streets or in the markets for sale. They have never been cured nor assorted. They are in no condition to be shipped. They cannot be long kept in such a condition. The huckster or buyer sees this, takes advantage of circumstances, sometimes combining with others of his class to put down the price, picks out the most indifferent fruit, and offers for the whole a price based upon this inferior sample. So far as the producer is concerned the fruit is sacrificed, and especially if the market be full. The grower should never put himself at the mercy of such men, for even the tender mercies of such men are cruel. If the grower will so gather, assort, and pack his fruit that it will keep for weeks or for months, as may be done, he need not be driven to such sacrifices.

As the fruit of a grove begins to ripen, let the gardener pass through, and, taking tree by tree, take from it all fruit that shows such defects as will lead him to conclude that it will never come to perfection. Let him gather all specked fruit. This can be done week after week, always selecting the ripest of such fruit. As such is the first to ripen there is always a market for it, and, rightly managed, at a paying price. If such fruit is allowed to remain on the tree it will get no better, and its presence will damage the fruit which should remain longer on the tree. Before the better oranges begin to ripen the gardener should be well acquainted with the quality of the fruit of each tree, so that he can classify them according to quality of flavor, from the acid to the sweet, from the dry to the juicy, and various varieties. In gathering, cut the stem close to the orange, handle in boxes containing not more than 75 or 100, which boxes place on shelves in the packing-house until the surplus moisture has escaped from the rind, leaving it tough and pliable. This drying process will require not more than five days. *Always select a dry day on which to gather the fruit.* When the orange is thoroughly ripe—during and after January—its hold on the stem is not so tenacious ; it can then be plucked more expeditiously without the aid of the knife, a skilful hand with a practical double jerk being able to break the stem in the eye with no danger of tearing the skin.

The boxes for packing should be of light material, neatly made, tolerably close, and hooped. Dimensions 12 x 12 x 27, with partition in the middle. In making these, one side should be left open. In packing, the open side should be turned up, and the box lined with sheets of paper laid on the bottom and resting against the side. Each orange should be wrapped separately in tissue-paper containing as little oil as possible, so that it will readily absorb and throw off moisture. The wrapper should be careful to reject every bruised or otherwise injured orange. The packer should be careful not to put different varieties in the same box. The buyer should know when he has tasted any orange from a box or brand that all others of the same brand or box are its equal. In packing, the oranges should be placed closely together in layers, so that there can be no rolling or sliding of the fruit in the box. The last layer should project one fourth of an inch above the sides of the box, so that the top when nailed on should hold the layers firmly in their places, even after there has been some shrinkage of the fruit. This is all-important when the fruit is to be transported a considerable distance, and especially when transported by rail. The box should now be marked with the number of oranges and the brand of the fruit.

In shipping, water transportation should be preferred to rail, especially during the first part of the trip, as such transportation is not so apt to jar and rub the fruit as rail. When the producer knows a *responsible* merchant who will buy his fruit and sell it by retail, it is better for him to make the arrangement with him to furnish him oranges at a stipulated price for each brand throughout the season. It will lessen the expense of a commission to a third party; besides, commission merchants as a class have not dealt fairly with the Florida fruit and vegetable grower. Bad packing, poor transportation, and dishonest commission merchants have done more to keep back the progress of Florida and discourage fruit and vegetable growing than any other three causes combined. And of the three the dishonest commission merchant has made himself the largest but the lowest of these evils. There are some honorable exceptions, and such should be liberally patronized. But it is a vocation offering such opportunities for rascality and such bribes for dishonesty, it would be well for the producer to be cautious as to whom he makes consignments.

Transportation from Florida to the North and

North-west is yet inadequate, and the lines already in existence are badly managed ; many of the officers on these lines have not done their duty to their employers, and they have done much to discourage fruit and vegetable growing in Florida. This grave charge can be proved by a multitude of facts. A few should be mentioned, to show something of their general character. Some crates of strawberries, to be packed in ice and destined for New York, were thrown upon deck after the manner of a traveller's trunk. Remonstrance was made by the owner. "Got angel in dar?" was the ready reply of the deck-hand, emphasizing his wit with an additional thump of the crate. The captain of the boat laughed at the wit of the negro, and left him to repeat his damage and wit on the next victim who should take the pains to grow fruit for such fun. About thirty-three per cent of the melons which are shipped from the St. Johns to New York never reach their destination. There is no excuse for this. The watermelon, well cared for and handled, will easily keep from six to ten days. A cargo of twenty thousand melons shipped from Fernandina to New York reached the latter port well cooked. Unfortunately it is not the fashion to eat cooked melons. West and Middle Florida should have direct communication with the North-west. That beautiful, rich, and attractive country would in a few years become like the garden of the Lord. This is a seeming digression from orange culture, but it is pardonable ; for while the orange is not so perishable as some other things needing transportation, the increasing production is such as will demand, in addition to semi-weekly lines of steamers from Fernandina and Jacksonville to New York, a daily orange train from Florida to the North-west.

CHAPTER XXIII.

CROPS THAT MAY BE GROWN AMONG THE ORANGE TREES.

THE question is often asked, "How can I make a living while the orange trees are coming into bearing?" The answer is, "Just as you would make a living if you were doing nothing else but farming or gardening, or growing fruits that come in bearing sooner than the orange." If you are a city clerk, and know nothing about hoeing and plowing and chopping, you would find it rather tough, for the first year or two, to make your bread in the valley of the Nile, or your meat and bread in the blue-grass region of Kentucky. In either case you would have to deny yourself, for a year or two, of "luxuries" dear to you, among the most valued of these, *otium cum dignitate*. You would have to pull off your coat and go to work. You would have to consult the natives to learn practical and common sense, and you would be surprised at the profound depth of your ignorance of the means of making the bread you have been eating all your life. But knowledge, even this humble knowledge, is good for the soul and the man. And you can learn, and even learn to love to work. The sweet sleep and refreshing rest under the soothing anodyne of labor would come without the learning. After a while would come the noble independence of a *free man*. Try it, young man, try it! Come from the crowded city to the country! Come South, come to Florida! You will regret it for the first year or two, and apply hard names to your adviser, think him and his book a great humbug; but if you have the virtue of continuance you will after a while bless him for the advice, and your children will bless you for your wisdom. But from this digression to the subject in hand.

It has already been noticed that garden crops may be grown among the trees profitably to the laborer and the trees. Grapes and figs can be brought into bearing within three years from the cutting, and peaches in three years from the seed. Guavas can be grown under shade of trees in the latitude of St. Augustine, and abundantly and profitably farther South. Plums do better in Florida than anywhere I have ever seen them grow. The Japan and wild-goose plum will bear transportation to Northern cities. They are both excellent fruits and bring a good price. Sweet potatoes can be grown in young groves. But as they require deep cultivation and to be planted in ridges, the rows should not run too near the orange trees. Sugar-cane can be planted profitably, but should never be planted among orange trees. The smaller varieties of Indian corn can be profitably grown among the orange trees, both for bread and forage. It is better, however, to grow it for forage, as it is not so exhaustive to land when cut in a green state. Indeed the names of crops that may be grown profitably, if the land is kept rich, is legion ; as our climate and soil will grow almost everything that can be grown in the temperate zone as well as all the semi-tropical plants. Sheep and poultry can be raised with great profit in Florida. In almost every neighborhood sheep will find an excellent range in the pine forest. They should be penned at nigh in the grove. For this purpose a movable pen of light boards four inches wide, the sections of twenty and sixteen feet in length, so that when sections are put together they will be self-supporting, is a great convenience. The writer has one such which requires only a few moments to move, so that stock penned can have fresh land on which to rest every night or two. It is a good way to fertilize a grove, if the pen is not allowed to remain too long in one place. A similar arrangement can be had for poultry, so that they can always be confined at the right spot. If too heavy to lift, they can be made to roll on wheels made of sections of a round log.

CHAPTER XXIV.

OILS, PERFUMES, EXTRACTS, ETC., FROM THE CITRUS.

THE subjects mentioned above need to be carefully considered by the orange growers of Florida. In Europe the manufacture of these products of the citrus is about equal in value to the exported fruit. Essential oil is distilled from the tender shoots, rinds of the fruit, and leaves of the trees. The most delicate perfumes and oils are obtained from the flowers, especially from the flower of the wild orange. Marmalade is made from the sour fruit, citric acid and concentrated lemon-juice from the lemon, while the citron yields that most delicate conserve bearing the same name, for which we pay high prices. Many of these delicate and truly valuable products of the orange can be prepared on the orange plantation at comparatively little cost. It would be better if some enterprising firm would locate at Jacksonville or some other orange centre, and combine in one establishment all these interests. There would be no difficulty in obtaining ample material for a large establishment, even thus early in our orange growing. These materials—leaves, tender shoots, flowers, young fruit dropped, imperfect fruit, and sour fruit—would alone, if such an establishment were erected, pay for the cultivation of the grove and leave the fruit as a clear gain.

Such a business would be a source of vast wealth to the firm which should engage in it with sufficient capital and skill. These articles manufactured from the citrus would be put in a durable form and made ready for exportation to any part of the world. With this profit added to the profit arising from the sale of the fruit, at one cent for the orange and half a cent for the lemon, the citrus crop in Florida alone could, in a score of years, be made to exceed the value of the entire cotton crop grown in the South. Florida certainly has a bright future before her if her sons are wise enough to labor for that future. In her broad acres there is ample room, not only for her natural and adopted sons, but for the hundreds of thousands of their fellow-citizens to whom these sons of Florida extend a hearty invitation to come and occupy with them these broad acres, this genial climate, and this vast wealth, enough for all, and quite as good as can be found this side of Heaven.

CHAPTER XXV.

DISEASES OF THE ORANGE IN FLORIDA.

SINCE the early editions of this work some progress has been made in the successful treatment of the diseases affecting the orange. The author has been careful to read all that has been written, and to keep up his habit of observation and experiments in the interest of the growers of the orange. This short chapter is added for their benefit and at the request of many growers.

I. BLIGHT.

The disease now most threatening and least understood is the leaf blight or curl. I first observed this disease near Apopka City, in Orange County, Fla., during the year 1872. Having with me a glass of high magnifying power I was led to suspect the cause. The microscope established me in my convictions.

The cause, a microscopic fungus, so minute that it cannot seriously affect the large branches, as it cannot send its roots deep enough to interfere with the tubes of circulation. Its damage to the smaller branches is done by filling the tubes, for conveying the sap from the roots to the leaves and smaller branches, so full of the roots of the fungus as to first impede and then to entirely stop the flow of sap to the extremities of the branches and leaves, so that death comes to these from strangulation.

Remedies.—First cut off all branches of less than an inch in diameter. Next spray the tree and neighboring trees—to prevent the spread of germs —with some solution of sulphur—sulphate of lime, five pounds to forty gallons of water; sulphate of iron, copperas, one pound to forty gallons of water. This spraying should be kept up occasionally till you are convinced that the germs of the disease are killed. Broadcast over the ground pulverized copperas at the rate of one hundred pounds to the acre.

A friend to whom I gave some years ago this prescription, thinks that he hastened the cure by lifting the bark of the trunk and applying the flower of sulphur. His success was complete.

II. DIE-BACK.

The symptoms of this disease are so marked and so characteristic that nothing needs to be added on this point beyond what has already been said in this volume.

Causes.—Excess of nitrogenous fertilizers will produce the die-back. Proximity of trees to stables or cowpens, deposits of slops from house, chicken pens, the roosting of fowls in the trees, excess of muck, the decay of masses of roots in the ground near the trees, are all frequent causes of die-back.

Remedies.—Prune the roots till all blackened wood is cut off. Do not cultivate, but let the ground grow in weeds or grass till the cause is removed. The soil will be greatly improved by a liberal application of lime.

III. FOOT-ROT.

(*Gum disease, mal di goma*).—This disease has long been known in Europe. The prominent symptoms are exudation of a gummy or sappy fluid from near the base of the trunk, the decay of the bark in that region and of the roots below. Beginning at one or more points, the disease extends in all directions till the tree is girdled. Sometimes the exudation of diseased sap appears at various places along the trunk. This disease, like most others, is apt to attack trees enfeebled by age or bad condition of the soil, etc.

Causes.—Rupture of bark admitting the atmosphere charged with germs of ferment. Piles of litter at the base of the trunk would prove a favorable place for the development of such germs. The disease is most prevalent after a freeze sufficient to rupture the bark of the trunk. The decaying of fruit or other vegetable matter upon the ground furnish the germs of the disease, while the oxidation of the sap and the slow circulation resulting from damage by the cold favor the conditions for rapid development of acidity, and the tree is affected as an animal suffering from blood-poison. So soon as the sap begins to ferment it attracts various insects. If the disease is at the base of the tree or in the crown roots the wood-lice are invited; if above the crown roots the beetles are attracted. The eggs of the latter soon develop into larva. Both classes of insects feed upon the sap, in its first (sweet) stage of fermentation, and so keep up the irritation, increasing the flow of sap from the wounds, and so help to extend and promote the diseases.

Remedies.—Alkalies to check fermentation and correct acidity, and some penetrating insecticide to destroy the insects that may be hiding beneath the loosened bark. The following has invariably proven effective if the disease has not progressed too far before taken in hand: Bring seven pounds of any washing soap to the boiling point, while boiling stir in one gallon of kerosene. Add sixty gallons of water. When this is to be used add lime to the consistency of a good whitewash. Cut away all the diseased bark and apply the whitewash liberally.

Preventives.—Keep the crown roots well exposed; keep litter from accumulating around the base of the trunk; keep standing water from around the trees and the grounds well drained. If the bark is damaged at any time by cold or by bruise, apply the above prepared whitewash.

The following paragraphs are taken from the *Journal of Mycology*, published by the Agricultural Department of the United States for 1891 :

IV. SCAB.

1. *Nature of the Disease.*—This disease first makes its appearance in the form of whitish or cream-colored spots, more commonly on the under side of the leaf, but often on the upper side, and occasionally on the young twigs and fruit. Those on the leaf are often accompanied by a depression or pit on the opposite side. These spots grow larger and often coalesce ; ultimately they turn dark, and if abundant the leaf becomes badly curled, twisted, or otherwise distorted, and more or less covered with the wart-like eruptions which the disease has developed.

2. *Distribution.*—The disease is widespread ; in a few localities it does not seem to be regarded as anything serious. In other localities, where it is more abundant, it is becoming the source of much alarm. It is not confined to young trees, but attacks equally young and old stock. While more abundant on the wild orange it is by no means confined to it, nor even to sour stock. We saw it on wild orange trees very commonly, on grape fruit and lemon trees frequently, and on sweet orange trees rarely.

3. *Causes.*—Professor F. L. Scribner, who made

a study of this disease in 1886,* attributed it to a parasitic fungus (a species of *Cladosporium*), whose growth in the tissues of the leaf produced the distortions and sapped its vitality. Our own observations confirmed these conclusions.

4. *Remedies.*—In the paper above alluded to Professor Scribner makes the following recommendations for spraying mixtures: (*a*) A solution of potassium bisulphide, one half ounce to the gallon; (*b*) liquid grison; (*c*) one half pint carbolic acid and one pound of glycerine added to ten gallons strong soap-suds.

We could not learn that these remedies or any other treatment had been attempted in any of the orange regions visited.

V. LEAF-SPOT.

1. *Nature of Disease.*—On certain leaves of the orange, both wild and sweet, faded spots appear, varying in shape, but mostly rounded or oval, and in size from one eighth of an inch to an inch in diameter. As the disease progresses, these spots become grayish brown and dead, and covered on one or both surfaces with a series of minute black points, which contain the fruit of the fungus, which is the cause of the disease.

2. *Distribution.*—This disease was found at only

---

* Bulletin Torrey Botanical Club, xiii., 181-83 (October, 1886).

one point in Lake County. Dr. Martin found it in 1886 at Green Cove Spring. It does not seem to be widespread nor at present of much importance, but is recorded here that attention may be called to it, so that its nature may be known and its progress watched.

3. *Cause.*—The cause of this disease is a parasitic fungus (*Colletotrichum adustum*, Ellis) which draws the nourishment from the leaf it inhabits. It belongs to a group of fungi that are known to be imperfect forms, and are supposed to be a phase of growth in the life history of some mature form of fungus. The particular form of which this species is a phase of growth is not known nor even suspected. Its connections are to be looked for among some of the many species of ascomycetous fungi which inhabit decaying vegetable matter, and for this reason are supposed by the uninformed to be of no economic interest.

VI. SOOTY MOULD.

1. *Nature of the Disease.*—The leaves of certain trees badly affected with some kind of scale insects become covered with a sooty layer, which is of a dark drab or dirt color early in its growth and finally becomes sooty black. The layer thus formed is only loosely attached to the smooth surface of the orange leaf and frequently comes off in patches.

2. *Distribution.*—This disease does not appear to

be very widespread on the orange-trees in Florida, and the material collected was young and immature. We found it, however, more abundant on *Magnolia fœtida*, *Smilax* sp., and other shrubs which were abundantly affected with scale insects.

3. *Causes.*—In 1876 Dr. W. G. Farlow published an elaborate paper giving a full account of this disease as affecting the orange and olive trees of California, and referring it to a fungus (*Capnodium citri*, Berk. & Desm.) which feeds on the honey dew produced by the bark-lice. While the fungus draws no nourishment from the orange leaves themselves, it must, if abundant, seriously interfere with the process of assimilation, and therefore be regarded as injurious.

4. *Remedies.*—In the paper above mentioned, spraying with a strong solution of alkali soap is recommended. The disease has not yet made sufficient progress in Florida to demand much treatment, and with the natural enemies of the scale insect to check their development is not likely to prove a serious difficulty.

CHAPTER XXVI.

CONCLUSION.

TO those who are thinking of engaging in this important branch of industry, I would say a few words in concluding. It is evident that Florida is destined to take the lead as a fruit-growing State. Land is rapidly increasing in value. The sooner you buy the better. But before purchasing, learn all you can of the different portions of the State. If possible, travel over it with an eye to finding that section which will best suit you, so that after locating you will never be made to regret your first choice. Each portion has its advantages. Middle Florida has fertile soils, and with its rolling lands is perhaps the most beautiful section of the State. The orange has received too little attention in Middle Florida. Those who have made the attempt with proper care and protection have grown fine oranges there.

The country through which the St. Johns River flows, having at once one of the grandest streams in America, and with it ample facilities for transportation, has, as yet, attracted the most attention. The eastern shore of this river, especially, is admirably adapted to the culture of the orange. Being protected from the severe north-westerly winds by this wide expanse of water, it is as little liable to the injuries of frost as counties one hundred miles farther south. The counties in the lower portion of the State have generally fine lands, and grow the orange successfully.

Having settled, plant your grove of one or more acres; let the size be determined by your means, never undertaking more than you can keep in the highest state of cultivation. As to choosing between the budded and seedling tree, decide as you wish fruit sooner or later. A budded grove would perhaps best suit a man well advanced in age. If, however, the seedling is your choice, make yourself entirely satisfied as to the quality of the orange from which the seed were taken, and also the remoteness of the original tree from trees bearing fruit of poor quality. Better plant the seed yourself and wait, rather than have doubt on this point. Keep the land rich and *thoroughly* tilled. The best remedy for drouth is to have the plow and cultivator or sweep continually going. It is a great mistake to plow only with respect to the grass. The intervals between cultivating should not be so great as to give the grass an opportunity for growing. Where the ground is frequently stirred there will be fewer insects, their eggs, which are often deposited in the earth, not being permitted to hatch. Examine your trees often and closely. If insects attack them, treat at once. Study your soil, note what it is deficient in, and supply the deficiency.

Your grove having come into bearing, your toil is over and your fortune made. You can now have the pleasure of eating this most healthful of fruits of your own raising. An eminent physician has said that if each of his patients would eat an orange in the morning before breakfast, his practice would soon be gone. If France is sought by the invalid for the grape cure, Florida will be resorted to for the orange cure as well as for its unrivalled climate.

Do not be afraid of glutting the market with the orange; it can never be done. There are thousands of persons who have never seen an orange, and many more who have to pay exorbitant prices for them where they are rarely seen. If there is a supply the demand will be created. When Florida's oranges are counted by the hundred million she will have adequate means for transporting them to the best markets and to *all* markets, without a doubt. The people of this country know very little about eating the orange. They have not yet acquired a taste for this queen of all fruits.

If the orange growers of Europe find it profitable to send their indifferent fruit to us, after having to pay a tariff (for which we are indebted to General Sanford of this State), how much better can we afford to sell at home, even for the same price.

The above-named gentleman, after his tour through the orange-growning portions of Europe, states that they claim to be able to raise the orange profitably when getting only one dollar per thousand, their average price now being about three dollars per thousand. Is there any probability of the luscious Florida orange being reduced to this price, even if her market be restricted to the limits of America? But the day is not far distant when our oranges will be found on the tables of the rich in Europe in preference to the inferior fruit they now get there.

The orange grower should not be contented with his *present* knowledge. This is a progressive age; orange culture is in its infancy. If we would keep well posted we should study our vocation no less diligently than others do theirs. The papers of the State have done much good in this direction, giving the successes and results of experiments of different men. Every orange grower should take the paper published in his own section; these papers should have a department devoted specially to fruit growers, who should make it a repository for mutual information.

Finally, to be successful, the fruit grower must watch and work; but not always, for soon golden harvests may be had for the gathering.

APPENDIX.

GALLESIO ON THE ORANGE.

IN his valuable and standard work on "The Citrus Family," which I have already quoted from several times in the preceding pages, Gallesio gives the following highly interesting account of the origin of the orange and its introduction into Europe:

The orange and lemon tree were unknown to the Romans; therefore they could only have been indigenous in a country where this great people had never penetrated. We all know the vast extent of this empire, yet commercial relations extend themselves always far beyond political bounds. If these trees had been cultivated in places open to the traffic of the Romans, these fruits would have become at once the delight of the tables of Rome, given up to luxury. They could not, then, have been cultivated at this period, except in the remote parts of India, beyond the Ganges. The north of Europe and of Asia, it is true, were equally unknown to the Romans, but their climates were not at all suited to these plants. The interior and west coasts of Africa, although in great part deserts, and destitute of the moisture necessary to the orange, inclosed, nevertheless, fertile districts where it might have thriven. But the state of culture of the tree at the present time in that country, and the historic facts proving to us that it was not naturalized there till long after, make us certain that it was entirely unknown there as well as in Europe. It is true, that at the time of the discovery of the Cape of Good Hope, the Portuguese found many citrons and bigarades upon the eastern coast of Africa, and in the part of Ethiopia where Romans had never penetrated ; but they found these trees only in gardens, and in a state of domesticity, and we do not know but that the Arabs, who had cultivated them in Egypt, in Syria, and in Barbary, had penetrated into these countries in the first years of their conquests. There remains, then, for us only to seek the native country of the orange in Southern Asia—that is to say, in those vast countries known under the general name of East Indies. But these regions were in part known to the Romans, who, since the discovery of the monsoons, made by Hippalus, carried their maritime commerce as far as Muziro (Massera, an island off the south-east coast of Arabia), by way of the Red Sea, the navigation of which employed a great number of vessels, and whose commerce, according to Pliny, should have been valued at fifty million sesterces ($2,000,000) per annum. Their fleets had penetrated even to Portum Gebenitarum, which appears to have been the present Ceylon ;

and, although these voyages cost them five years of fatigue and danger, nevertheless the thirst for gold and luxury of Rome had multiplied to the last degree the vessels engaged in this trade. We must believe, then, that the lemon and orange did not exist in all that part of the country this side of the Indus, and perhaps not even in all the part lying between that river and the Ganges ; otherwise these fruits would have been extolled by the Roman merchants, where the citron was so much valued ; and we should find at least some mention made of them in narratives and voyages descended to us from those ancient times. If we consult the description of the coasts of India, from the river Indus to the Euphrates, which we have in the voyage of Nearchus, one of Alexander's captains ; that of the Troglodytes, and coasts of the Indian Sea, by Arianus, the voyage of Iambolus, reported by Diodorus of Sicily, where he gives a description of an isle of the Indian Sea unknown before him, where he had been thrown by a storm ; or, finally, the Indian voyage of Pliny---we find not the least indication of either orange, or even citron ; yet Nearchus carefully notes the plants found in his course, and speaks of palms, myrtles, and vines ; of wheat, and generally of all the trees of Asia except the olive. Arianus enlarges upon the vegetable productions of those districts, giving the descriptions of those found in public roads.

Iambolus saw in the unknown island, which appears to have been Sumatra, a grain that we recognize as maize, which has been introduced into Europe since the passage round the Cape of Good Hope. We must then admit that the lemon and orange trees could not have originated but in the region beyond the Ganges, and that, in early centuries of the empires of the Cæsars, they had not yet been brought from those climates where they were indigenous. They increased perhaps still without culture in the midst of the woods, the hand of man not having yet appropriated them as ornaments for his garden. But this event could not long be delayed. The beauty of the tree, and the facility with which it reproduced itself, would naturally extend the culture to adjoining provinces, and the European, quick to seize the productions of all the rest of the globe, would not fail to enrich himself from these regions.

Facts prove that this result has been reached, but we know not the date of passage, or the circumstances favoring it. We will now make this the object of our researches. The Romans, at the time of Pliny, had extended their commerce on the side of India as far as it was ever carried during the empire; the power of Rome, instead of increasing, only became weaker from this period; and the fall of the Western portion was accompanied in Europe by the decay of letters, art, agriculture, and commerce. In this general overturn, the Greeks preserved, it is true, with a taste for arts and luxury, some relations with India, but trade with those countries had never taken other course than by way of the Red Sea, and this was closed from the seventh century by the Arabian invasion of Egypt, which soon followed the invasion of Arabia by the barbarians of the west (Ethiopians).

The commerce of these rich lands must then have taken a much longer and more dangerous route. The traders were obliged, after going down the Indus, to reascend that stream, and by the Bactrea (Bolkh) to reach the Oxus, and finally, by the last pass into the Caspian Sea, from whence they went into the Black Sea by the river Don. But this long and dangerous voyage was never undertaken by the traders of Constantinople; they would not have been able to traverse with safety such an extent of country, partly a desert, and in part inhabited by wandering tribes, most of them nations with whom they were nearly always at war, who were destined in the end to swallow the Greek Empire.

They therefore limited themselves to receiving upon the borders of the Caspian Sea the merchandise of India, brought to them by intermediate people. One can scarcely realize that in such a state of affairs the orange tree could pass into Europe, for this beautiful part of the world had never been in so general disorder or had so little intercourse with India. Her luxury and commerce were nearly annihilated, and the Arabians, whom the new religion of Mahomet rendered fanatics and conquerors, menaced on one side the tottering empire of the Greeks, and on the other threatened to plunge into barbarism the West, just beginning to be civilized. Yet it was precisely at this point of time, and by the conquering spirit of this people, that the great changes were prepared which should revive and extend farther than ever before the commercial relations of Europe with Asia, and of Asia herself with the more distant regions of her own continent.

The Arabs, placed in a country which binds together three grand divisions of the globe, have extended their conquests into Asia and Africa much farther than any people before them. Masters of the Red Sea and Mediterranean, they had invaded all the African Coast this side of Atlas, and penetrated beyond to the region of the Troglodytes (Ethiopians living in caves), the ancient limit of the Roman establishments on the east coast of this continent; they had made settlements there, and according to the testimony of a historian of the country, cited by Barros, they had populated in the fourth century of the Hegira (A. D. 944) the towns of Brava, Mombas, and Quiloa, whence they extended themselves to Sofalo, Melinda, and to the islands of Bemba, Zanzibar, Monfra, Comoro, and St. Laurent. On the side of Asia they had carried their conquests, in the third century of the Hegira, to the extremities of the Relnahar, and toward the middle of the fourth century, under the Selucidæ, they had established a colony at Kashgar, the usual route of caravans to Toorkistan or to China, and which, according to Albufeda (a geographer and historian of Damascus), is situated in longitude 87° (73° 57'), consequently they had penetrated very far into Asia.

Never had there been in Asia an empire so vast, and never had the commerce of nations so near Europe been pushed so far into India.

A position thus advantageous and favorable to the commercial spirit and love of luxury which succeeded, among the Arabs, the fury of conquest, would naturally cause them to learn of and to appropriate many exotic plants peculiar to the regions they had conquered, or to the adjoining countries. Fond of medicine and agriculture, in which they have specially excelled, and of the pleasures of the open country, in which they have always delighted, they continued to profit with eagerness from the advantages offered by their settlements, and the hot climates which they inhabited. Indeed, it is to them that we owe the knowledge of many plants, perfumes, and Oriental aromatics, such as musk, nutmegs, mace, and cloves.

It was the Arabs who naturalized, in Spain, Sardinia, and Sicily, the cotton-tree of Africa and the sugar-cane of India ; and in their medicines we for the first time hear of the chemical change known as distillation, which appears to have originated in the desire to steal from nature the perfumes of flowers and aroma of fruits.

It is then not surprising that we are indebted to them for the acclimatization of the orange and lemon trees in Syria, Africa, and some European islands. It is certain that the orange was known to their physicians from the commencement of the fourth century of the Hegira. The Damascene has given in his Antidotary the recipe for making oil with oranges, and their seeds (*oleum de citrangula, et oleum de citrangulorum seminibus.* Mat. Silv., f. 58), and Avicenna, who died in 428 of the Hegira (1050), has added the juice of the bigarade to his syrup of *alkedere et succi acetositatus citri* (otrodj), *et succi acetositatis citranguli* (narendg)." These two Arabians seem to have first employed it in medicine.

I have examined with care the authors of this nation who preceded these, and find in no other the least hint relating to these species. Mesue, even, who speaks of the citron, says not a word of orange or lemon. I have observed, on the contrary, that Avicenna, in giving his recipe for making syrup of alkedere, in which he puts juice of the bigarade, announces it as a composition of his own invention. This circumstance would indicate that this fruit had been known but a short time in Persia, but it suffices that it was cultivated there to prove that it might, at once, pass into Irak (probably Irak-Arabee, in Asiatic Turkey, comprising Bagdad), and into Syria.

These countries, which joined, were also connected by political ties, which facilitate communication, and their inhabitants were more civilized then than before or since. A passage by Massoudi, reported by the learned M. de Sacy in the notes to his translation of Abd-Allatif, a writer of the twelfth century of our era, seems to confirm our ideas upon this subject, and to determine the date of this event. It accords with all the data just given, and with historic facts that we have collected. He expresses himself thus : " The round citron *otrodj modawar* was brought from India since the year 300 of the Hegira. It was first sowed in Oman (part of Arabia), from thence carried to Irak (part of Old Persia) and Syria, becoming very common in the houses of Tarsus and other frontier cities of Syria, at Antioch, upon the coasts of Syria, in Palestine, and in Egypt. One knew it not before, but it lost much of the sweet odor and fine color which it had in India, because it had not the same climate, soil, and all that which is peculiar to that country." The lemon appeared perhaps a little later in these different countries, for we see no mention of it either in the Damascene or in Avicenna, but its description meets our eye in all the works of Arabian writers of the twelfth century, especially Ebn-Beitar, who has given to it an article in his dictionary of simple remedies. The Latin translation of this article was published in Paris in 1702 by Andres

Balunense. The Imperial Library contains several manuscripts of this dictionary.

I had thought to have found proof that the lemon was known by the Arabs in the ninth century, having seen in a history of India and China, dated 238 of the Hegira (A.D. 860); of which a French translation was printed in Paris in 1718, the writers had spoken of the lemon as a fruit found in China. But M. de Sacy, who examined the original, ascertained that the word *limon* was inserted by the translator. In the Arabian text one finds only that of *otrodj*, which signifies merely *citron*. Therefore this history, far from proving that the Arabs knew the lemon tree at this period, proves quite the contrary. It was not until the tenth century of our era that this warlike people enriched with these trees the garden of Oman (in South-eastern Arabia), whence they were propagated in Palestine and Egypt. From these countries they passed into Barbary and Spain, perhaps also into Sicily.

Leon of Ostia tells us that in 1002 a prince of Salerna presented citrine apples (*poma citrina*) to the Norman princes who had rescued him from the Saracens.

The expression *poma citrina*, used by this author, appears to me to designate fruit like the citron rather than the citron itself, then known under the name of *citri*, or of *mala medica*.

It is thus that we should recognize the orange in the *citron rond* spoken of by Massoudi in a passage already quoted.   This conjecture accorded with known events and data. The Arabs invaded Sicily about the beginning of the ninth century (828), the orange was taken from India to Arabia after the year 300 of the Hegira—that is to say, early in the ninth century of our era. The citrine apples of Leon d'Ostia dates from 1002, and were regarded as objects rare and precious enough to be offered as gifts to princes. Thus we have between its introduction into Arabia and propagation in Sicily an interval of nearly a century. In order to conform to the expression of Massoudi, let us suppose that the orange tree was brought from Arabia some thirty or forty years later—say about 330 of Hegira. If we allow fifty years for its propagation in Palestine, Egypt, and Barbary, and finally twenty years for its naturalization in Sicily, we fill precisely the interval between one epoch and the other.

A passage in the history of Sicily, by Nicolas Specialis, written in the fourteenth century, gives still more probability to this opinion.

This writer, in recounting the devastation by the army of the Duke of Calabria in 1383, in the vicinity of Palermo, says that it did not spare even the trees of sour apples *pommes acides*, called by the people *arangi*, which had adorned since old time, the royal palace of Cubba. (Nicolas Specialis, bk. 7, c. 17.)

The name Cubba given to this royal pleasure-house seems to refer to the time of the Arabic rule;

it is probably derived from the Arabic word Cobbah, meaning vault or arch ; perhaps some grand dome upon this country-house gave the place its name.

These data, however, do not appear to me sufficiently strong to combat the authority of a very reliable historian, who says expressly that the lemon and the orange trees were not known in Italy or France or in other parts of Christian Europe in the eleventh century. Such are the words of Jacques de Vitry, in speaking of Syrian trees in his history of Jerusalem. The testimony of this bishop, who ought to have known these countries, would appear to have more weight than simple conjectures based upon reasonings from analogy. Whatever be the authority of this historian, compared with the presumptions advanced by us with regard to Sicily, it will always be decisive respecting Lake Garda and the coasts of Liguria and Provence.

There is not a doubt that in these last-named countries the lemon and orange were unknown, not only in the tenth but even in the eleventh century. But an extraordinary event, destined to change the face of Europe, was to open anew to the people of the West the entrance to Syria and Palesstine. This was also the time when the Crusades, which began at the close of the eleventh century (1096), reawakened among Europeans the spirit of commerce and a taste for arts and luxury.

The Crusaders entered Asia Minor as conquerors, and thence spread themselves as traders into all parts of Asia. They were not mere soldiers, but brave men drawn from their families by religious enthusiasm, and who, in consequence, would hold fast to their country and their homes. They could not see without coveting these charming trees which embellished the vicinity of Jerusalem, with whose exquisite fruits nature has favored the climates of Asia.

It was, indeed, at this time that Europe enriched its orchards by many of these trees, and that the French princes carried into their country the damson, the St. Catharine (a pear), the apricot from Alexandria, and other species indigenous to those regions.

Sicilians, Genoese, and Provincials transported to Salerno, St. Remo, and Hyères the lemon and orange trees. Hear what a historian of the thirteenth century says to us on this subject; he had been in Palestine with the Crusaders, and his word should have great weight.

Jacques de Vitry expressed himself thus: "Besides many trees cultivated in Italy, Genoa, France, and other parts of Europe, we find here (in Palestine) species peculiar to the country, and of which some are sterile and others bear fruit. Here are trees bearing very beautiful apples—the color of the citron—upon which is distinctly seen the mark of a man's tooth. This has given them the common name of *pomme d'Adam* (Adam's apple); others produce sour fruit, of a disagreeable taste (*pontici*), which are called *limons*. Their juice is used for seasoning food, because it is cool, pricks the palate, and provokes appetite. We also see cedars of Lebanon, very fine and tall, but sterile. There is a species of cedar called *cedre maritime*, whose plant is small but productive, giving very fine fruits, as large as a man's head. Some call them citrons, or *pommes citrons*. These fruits are formed of a triple substance, and have three different tastes. The first is warm, the second is temperate, the last is cold. Some say that this is the fruit of which God commanded in Leviticus: 'Take you the first day of the year the fruit of the finest tree.' We see in this country another species of citrine apples, borne by small trees, and of which the cool part is less and of a disagreeable and acid taste; these the natives call *orenges*."

Behold, then, the Adam's apple, the lemon, the citron, and the bigarade found in Palestine by the Crusaders, and regarded as new trees foreign to Europe!

This passage does not accord, as far as the citron is concerned, with what Palladius says. He tells us that this plant was, in his time, cultivated in Sardinia and in Sicily. But we see, by Jacques de Vitry, that the citron of Palestine was distinguished by the extraordinary size of its fruit, equal to a man's head, and it must be that this last was a variety unknown to Europe.

It is, indeed, only since this epoch that we find in European historians and writers upon agriculture any mention of these trees. Doubtless the Arabians had already naturalized them in Africa and Spain, where the temperature favored so much their growth. Doubtless Liguria is the part of Italy where the culture of the Agrumi has made most progress. We have certain testimony to this in the work of a doctor of medicine of Mantua, writing near the middle of the thirteenth century. He says :

"The lemon is one of the species of citrine apples, which are four in number. First, citron. Secondly, orange (*citrangulum*), of which we have spoken before. Thirdly, the lemon. Fourthly, the fruit vulgarly called *lima*. These four species are very well known, principally in Liguria. The lemon is a handsome fruit, of fine odor. Its form is more oblong than that of the orange, and, like the orange, it is full of a sharp acid juice, very proper for seasoning meats. They make of its flowers odoriferous waters, fit for the use of the luxurious.

"The trees of these four species are very similar, and all are thorned. The leaves of the citron and lime are larger and less deeply colored than those of the orange or lemon. The lemon is composed of four different substances, as well as the citron, lime, and orange. It has an outer skin, not as deep in color as that of the orange, but which has more of the white. It is hot and biting ; thus it shows its bitter taste. The second skin or pith, between the outer skin and the juice, is white, cold, and difficult to digest. The third substance is its juice, which is sharp and of a strong acid, which will expel worms, and is very cold. The fourth is the seed, which, like that of the orange, is warm, dry, and bitter." (See Mat. Silv., " Pandecta Medicinæ," fol. 125.)

This testimony of Silvaticus is strengthened by all the authors who have written upon the *citrus*. There is not one but is convinced that these trees were for a long time very rare in Italy and in France, and that Liguria alone has traded in them since they were first known there. Sicily and the kingdom of Naples cultivated, perhaps before the Ligurians, the citron and orange trees; but in spite of the advantages of climate, it was only as objects of curiosity, limited to some delightful spots. This fact is established by the manner in which most writers of the twelfth century express themselves on this subject. Hugo Falcandus, who wrote of the exploits of the Normans in Sicily, from 1145 to 1169, saw there *lumies* and *orangers*, and points them out as singular plants, whose culture was still very rare. (Hugo Falcandus. See Muratori, Rerum Italicarum Scriptores.)

Ebn-al-Awam, an Arabian writer upon agriculture at Seville, near the end of the twelfth century, and whose work, translated into Spanish, was published at Madrid in 1802, speaks as if the culture were very much extended in Spain. Abd-Allatif, who was contemporary with the last-named author, expresses himself in like manner, and describes also a number of varieties cultivated in his time in Egypt —a circumstance showing that these trees had greatly multiplied. Their progress was slower in Italy and France. It appears that the lemon tree, brought first into these parts as a variety of citron, was for a long time designated by European writers under the generic name of *citrus*, although in Italy and the South of France the people had known it from the beginning under the proper name of *limon* —a name which has come down to us without submitting to any change. In fact, we find it in botanical works called *citrus limon*, or *mala limonia*, and sometimes *citrus medica*. The last was indefinitely used to designate lemon, citron, and orange, and very often the genus *citrus*.

The orange appeared in Italy under the name of *orenges*, which the people modified, according to the pronunciations of the different sections, into *arangio*, *naranzo*, *aranza*, *aranzo*, *citrone*, *cetrangolo*, *melarancio*, *melangolo*, *arancio*. One meets successively all these names in works of the thirteenth, fourteenth, and fifteenth centuries, such as those of Hugo Falcandus, Nicolas Specialis, Blondus Flavius, Sir Brunetto Latini, Ciriffo Calvaneo, Bencivenni, Boccaccio, Giustiniani, Leandro Alberti, and several others. The Provençals also received this tree under the name of *orenges*, and have changed it from time to time, in different provinces, into *arrangi*, *airange*, *orenge*, and finally *orange*. (See Glossary of the Roman Language, by Roquefort.)

During several centuries the Latin authors found themselves embarrassed in designating this fruit, which had no name in that language. The first who spoke of it used a phrase indicating its characteristics, accompanying it with the popular name of *arangi*, Latinized into *orenges, arangias, arantium*.

Thus, Jacques de Vitry, who calls the oranges *poma citrina*, adds, "The Arabs call them *orenges*." And Nicolas Specialis designated them as *pommes aigres* (*acripomorum arbores*), observing that the people call them *arangias*. These have been followed by Blondus Flavius and many others. Matheus Silvaticus first gave to the orange the name of *citrangulum*, and this denomination seems to have been followed for a long time by physicians and translators of Arabic works, who have very generally adopted it for rendering the Arabic word *arindj*.

Thus, *citrangulum* was received for more than a century in the language of science. Finally, little by little, were adopted the vulgar Latinized names in use among other writers, such as authors of chronicles, etc., and they have written successively, *arangium, arancium, arantium, anarantium, nerantium, aurantium, pomen aureum*. The Greeks followed in the same steps. They have either Grecianized the name of *narenge*, which was in use among Syrian Arabs, or they received it from the Crusaders from the Holy Land, and have adopted it in their language, calling it *nerantzion*. These have, however, always been considered vulgar names, and in general the better Latin writers have made use of the generic name, *citrus*, for designating the Agrumi.

This usage, followed by most of the writers on history and chorography, often occasions uncertainty and difficulty in researches concerning the beginning of this culture in the different countries where these trees have been introduced. The use of it as seasoning for food, brought from Palestine to Liguria, to Provence, and to Sicily, penetrated to the interior of Italy and France. The taste for confections was propagated in Europe with the introduction of sugar, and this delicate food became at once a necessary article to men in easy circumstances, and a luxury upon all tables. It was, above all, as confections that the Agrumi entered into commerce, and we see by the records of Savona that they were sent into cold parts of Italy, where people were very greedy for them.

After having cultivated these species for the use made of their fruits, they soon cultivated them as ornaments for the gardens. The monks began to fill with these trees the courts of their monasteries, in climates suited to their continual growth, and soon one found no convent not surrounded by them. Indeed, the courts and gardens of these houses show us now trees of great age, and it is said that the old tree, of which we see now a rejeton in the court of the convent of St. Sabina, at Rome, was planted by St. Dominic about the year 1200. This fact has no other foundation than tradition, but this tradition, preserved for many centuries, not only among the monks of the convent, but also among the clergy of Rome, is reported by Augustin Gallo, who, in 1559, speaks of this orange as a tree existing since time immemorial. If we refuse to attribute its planting to St. Dominic, we must at least refer it to a period soon after—that is, to the end of the thirteenth century, at the latest.

Nicolas Specialis, in the passage cited on another page, in describing the havoc made by the besiegers in the suburbs of Palermo, regrets the destruction of orangers, or trees of sour apples (*pommes aigres*), which he regards as rare plants, embellishing the pleasure-house of Cubba.

Blondus Flavius, a writer of the middle of the following century, speaks of the orange on the coast of Amalfi (a city of Naples) as a new plant, which as yet had no name in scientific language (Blond. Flav., Ital. Illus., p. 420); and he extols the valleys of Rapallo and San Remo, in Liguria, for the culture of the *citrus*, a rare tree in Italy. "Cugus ager (San Remo)," these are his words, "est citri, palmaquæ, arborum in Italia rarissirarum, ferax" (Blond. Flav., Ital. Illust., p. 296). Lastly, Pierre de Crescenzi, Senator of Bologna, who wrote in 1300 a treatise on agriculture, speaks only of the citron tree. We find in his expressions no hint of lemon or orange. The culture of these trees, then, had been begun in the fourteenth century only in a few places, but was extended in proportion as arts and luxury advanced the civilization of Europe.

The orange was from the first valued not alone for the beauty of its foliage and quality of its fruit, of which the juice was used in medicine, but also for the aroma of its flowers, of which essences were made. Pharmacists have employed with success the juice of the lemon in making medicines.

The orange tree must have been taken to Provence about the time it entered Liguria. It is to be presumed that the city of Hyères, so celebrated for the softness of its climate and the fertility of its soil, received it from the Crusaders, because from this port the expeditions to the Holy Land took their departure. We see, indeed, that it was greatly multiplied there, and in 1566 the plantations of oranges within its territory were so extensive and well grown as to present the aspect of a forest.

The territory of Nice, so advantageously placed between Liguria and Provence, would necessarily receive from its neighbors a tree so suited to the softness of its climate, sheltered by the Alps, and to the nature of its soil, fertilized by abundant waters. It appears that the culture had already greatly extended toward the middle of the fourteenth century, as we find in the history of Dauphiny that the Dauphin Humbert, returning from Naples in 1336, bought at Nice twenty plants of orange trees. (Hist. of Dauphiny, bk. 2, p. 271.)

From Naples and Sicily the orange and lemon trees must have been carried into the Roman States, into Sardinia and Corsica, and to Malta. The islands of the Archipelago perhaps first received them, because, belonging in great part to the Genoese and Venetians, it is probable they were the intermediate points whence the Crusaders of Genoa and Venice transported the plants to their homes. From these isles the trees afterward spread into the delightful coast of Salo on the shores of Lake Garda, where, in Gallo's time (1559), they were regarded as acclimated from time immemorial. Finally, the orange and the lemon penetrated into the colder latitudes, and perhaps one owes to the desire of enjoying their flowers and fruit the invention of hot-houses, afterward called orangeries. (The name of *orangerie* is a modern word in the French language. Olivier de Serre does not use it—he calls this kind of inclosure orange-houses (p. 633). The Italian language has no word responding precisely to orangery. We find in some modern authors, equivalent words, such as *aranciera, cedroniera, citronera*. (Fontana, Dizionario rustico, bk. 1, p. 74.) But the ancient writers styled these places for preserving these trees by the phrase, " Stanzone per i cedri." In Tuscany and the Roman States they call them *rimesse*. In other places they are known under the name of *serre* (inclosure). Matioli says that in his time they cultivated the oranges in Italy on the shores of the sea and of the most famous lakes, as well as in the gardens of the interior, but he says nothing of the places for sheltering them. Gallo speaks of rooms designed to receive the boxes of orange trees, which were very numerous at Brescia, but he does not designate them by any particular name. The Latin writers also used a periphrase. Ferraris calls an orangery *tectum hibernum*. Others call it *cella citraria*.)

This agricultural luxury was unknown in Europe before the introduction of the citron tree. We find not the least trace of it either in Greek or Latin writers.

It is true that from the time of the Emperor Tiberius in Rome they inclosed melons in certain portable boxes of wood, which were exposed to the sun in winter to make the fruit grow out of season. These inclosures were secured from the effects of cold by sashes or frames, and received the sun's rays through diaphanous stones (*specularia*), which held the place of our glass. But it seems they used no fire for heating them, and that they merely inclosed thus indigenous plants, of which they wished to force the fruiting out of season, it being a speculation of the cultivator rather than a luxurious ornament for embellishing the gardens. (Pliny, bk. 19, chap. 5, p. 336, and Columell, bk. 2, chap. 3, p. 42.) It is after the introduction of the citron tree into Europe that we begin to find among the ancients examples of artificial coverings and shelters against cold. Palladius is the first who speaks of these coverings, but only as appropriate for the citron, and gives no description of them. Florentin, who wrote probably after him, describes them at more length, and it seems by his expressions that in his time the citron was covered in the bad season by wooden roofs, which could be withdrawn when there was no occasion to defend them from cold, and which also could be arranged to secure for them the rays of the sun. (Florent., bk. 10, chap. 7, p. 219.)

This agricultural luxury, which began to appear about the time of Palladius and Florentin, must have been entirely destroyed in Italy by the invasion of the barbarians. I have remarked that Pierre de Crescenti, who wrote a treatise on agriculture in 1300, while treating of the citron, speaks only of walls to defend it from the north, and of some covers of straw. Brunsius and Antonius, quoted by Sprengel, have thought to find in the Statutes of Charlemagne indications of a hothouse. I have closely examined the article cited by those writers (in Comment. de reb. Franc. Orient, bk. 2, p. 902, etc.), but have not found a word that could make me believe this means of preserving delicate plants was employed at that period. I have even remarked that in these ordinances many plants are named which Charlemagne wished to have in his fields, but no word to be construed into ordering a shelter for any, unless the fig and almond. It is astonishing that, having spoken in detail of all the parts of the house, of laboring utensils the most ordinary, and even of those of housekeeping, he forgot an object of such great luxury as a hot-house. But in propoition as civilization and commerce increased riches and extravagance, the fruit of this tree became more sought for, and at the same time more common; while, above all, the properties of the new species just introduced extended its use in medicine, in agreeable drinks, and as a luxury of the table. At first they were in cold countries only a foreign production procured from the South, but afterward the people began to covet from the more happy climates the ornament of these trees, and to wish, above all, to embellish with them their gardens. In temperate climes they began to cultivate them in vases, depositing them during winter in caves; and in the cold latitudes the necessity of struggling against nature gave the idea of constructing apartments which could be heated at pleasure by fire, and which would shelter the plants from the rigor of the season.

It is difficult to fix the date at which they began to build edifices for protection of oranges. The oldest trace of it that I have been able to find is furnished by a passage in the history of Dauphiny, dated 1336. (We find in this history, printed at Geneva in 1722, an extract from an account of expenses made by Humbert, the Dauphin, in his voyage to Naples in 1336. In the expenses for the return we see the sum of ten tarins—the tarin was the thirtieth part of an ounce of Naples—for the purchase of twenty orange plants. "Item pro arboribus viginti de plantis arangiorum ad plantandum taren." X. Hist. of Daup., bk. 2, p. 276.) This, it is true, offers few circumstantial details for fixing the fact that the princes of Dauphiny had really, at that time, an orangery ; but as this historian tells us that Humbert bought at Nice twenty roots of oranges for a plantation (*ad plantandum*), it is to be supposed that he had in his palace at Vienna a place designed to preserve them in the winter ; for without this precaution they certainly would have perished in the rigorous climate of Dauphiny (in the south-west part of France.)

This luxury must have passed immediately into the capital of France, and though I have not yet found in history indications of these establishments before 1500, it is very probable that they were known there about the middle of the fourteenth century.

The celebrated tree, preserved still in the orangery at Versailles under the name of Francis First, or Grand Bourbon, was taken from the Constable of Bourbon in the seizure made of his goods in 1523. And this prince, who, it is said, possessed it for eighty years, could not have kept it except in an orangery. (The orange tree at Versailles, known as Francis Premier, is the most beautiful tree that I have seen in a box. It is twenty feet high, and extends its branches to a circumference of forty feet. Spite of that, I scarcely believe that this fine stalk dates from the fourteenth century. It is too vigorous, and the skin is too smooth, to be able to count so many years. It is probable that in so long a course of time it has been cut, and that the present tree is a sprout from the old root. This might have occurred after the frost of 1709, which penetrated even into sheltered places. One circumstance gives foundation to this conjecture. This tree is composed of two stalks, which both come out of the earth, and have a common stock. This is never the way the tree grows by nature, still less in a state of culture, and from roots held in vases. I have mostly remarked it in the greater number of trees growing upon a stump which had been razeed at the level of the ground. In such case one is forced to leave two suckers, because the sap, being very abundant, could not develop itself in one shoot. It would experience a sort of reaction, which would suffocate the stump and make it perish. This is a well-known fact in the South, where we cultivate largely the orange, and where the trees of double stems are generally recognized as rejetons, or suckers from old roots.)

After all these data we are authorized to think that in the fourteenth century they had begun already to erect buildings designed to create for exotic plants an artificial climate. But at the beginning of the fifteenth century orangeries passed from kings' gardens to those of the people, chiefly in countries where they were not compelled to heat them by fire, as in Brescia, Romagna, and Tuscany. (See Matioli, who says that in his day the orange was cultivated in Italy, in all the gardens of the interior, where certainly it could not live, unless in orangeries (Diosc. c. 132). We also find in Sprengel's History of Botany that in this country there were at that time many botanical gardens where they cultivated exotic plants—a circumstance which presupposes the necessity of hot-houses.)

About the middle of the seventeenth century this luxury was very general, and we see distinguished by their magnificence and grandeur the orangeries of the Farnese family at Parma; of the Cardinal Xantes; Aldobrandini and Pio, at Rome; of the Elector Palatine at Heidelberg (Oliv. de Ser., p. 633); of Louis XIII. in France; and even at Ghent, in Belgium, that of M. de Hellibusi, who imported plants from Genoa, and carried his establishment to the last degree of magnificence. (See Ferraris, p. 150, where he describes the orangery of M. de Hellibusi at Ghent, and that of Louis XIII. at Paris. The latter has been replaced by that of Versailles, of which the magnificence renders it perhaps the finest monument of this kind to be found in Europe.)

We now see orangeries in all the civilized parts of Europe, it being an embellishment necessary to all country-seats and houses of pleasure.

www.ingramcontent.com/pod-product-compliance
Lightning Source LLC
Chambersburg PA
CBHW020847160426
43192CB00007B/823